"Abanes has done a great service by setting the record straight on Rick Warren and Saddleback. Warren has a strong commitment to the core doctrines of the Christian faith and an unmistakable passion for reaching the lost, equipping pastors, and strengthening local churches. 'Purpose-driven' is not New Age, it's New Testament."

—James K. Walker,
President, Watchman Fellowship, Inc.

*God Bless*
*Alpha & Omega Investigations*

*Dorothy, Carla, Ashleigh &*
*The Boys*

# RICK WARREN
## *and the*
# PURPOSE
### *that*
# DRIVES
# HIM

## RICHARD ABANES

**HARVEST HOUSE PUBLISHERS**

EUGENE, OREGON

*Cover by Terry Dugan Design, Minneapolis, Minnesota*

For more information
about Richard Abanes and his work,
visit www.abanes.com

**RICK WARREN AND THE PURPOSE THAT DRIVES HIM**
Copyright © 2005 by Richard Abanes
Published by Harvest House Publishers
Eugene, Oregon 97402
www.harvesthousepublishers.com

Library of Congress Cataloging-in-Publication Data

Abanes, Richard.
    Rick Warren and the purpose that drives him / Richard Abanes.
            p. cm.
    Includes bibliographical references (p.        ) and index.
    ISBN-13: 978-0-7369-1738-4 (pbk.)
    ISBN-10: 0-7369-1738-1
    1. Warren, Richard, 1954–    2. Baptists—United States—Clergy—
Biography.    I. Title.
    BX6495.W37A24 2005
    286'.1'092—dc22                                                    2005010946

**Printed in the United States of America**

     05   06   07   08   09   10   11   12   13  /  BP-MS  /  10   9   8   7   6   5   4   3   2   1

# Contents

**Thanks to:**

Harvest House Publishers for believing in this book; Rick Warren and the leadership of Saddleback Church for their assistance with the project, including their cooperation in opening up church files to me; Kay Warren, for her invaluable help in checking the manuscript for accuracy and tone; Jeffrey Slipp, who assisted in making important editorial changes; David Chrzan, chief of operations at Saddleback Church, for helping me secure valuable information from a wide variety of sources; Chaundel Holladay, Tom Holladay, Jim Dobbs, and Anne Krumm; my friends for their support; my church family for their prayers; my fellow apologists for their guidance, encouragement, and suggestions. And Jesus Christ, the loving Savior and Lord of those who, in repentance, call upon His name and serve Him in newness of life, according to the eternal purposes of God. Maranatha!

# That Old-Time Religion

*When I humble myself and say, "God, break me.*
*I want to die to my ambitions. I want to surrender my*
*whole being for Your purpose"—that's a purpose-driven life.*
*"I want to surrender to Your purpose. For the rest of my life*
*from this day forward I want to go Your way. I want to be*
*purpose-driven, not profit-driven, not pleasing-other-people-driven,*
*but personally dedicated to You. I want to be purpose-driven."*

RICK WARREN, "LEADERSHIP CONFERENCE," PART 3,
SEPTEMBER 29, 2000

You were planned for God's pleasure."
"You were formed for God's family."
"You were created to become like Christ."
"You were shaped for serving God."
"You were made for a mission."[1]
These are God's five purposes for everyone, according to America's most recent mega-bestseller, *The Purpose-Driven Life* by Rick Warren, senior pastor of Saddleback Church (in Orange County, California). The book has "taken the country by storm" having sold more than 23 million copies since 2002, while

Warren, now called "America's Pastor,"[2] has attained celebrity status.

Warren's influence is almost unprecedented. As of early 2005, more than 400,000 pastors in 162 countries had been "trained in the 'church health' principles" he advocates.[3] And his e-mailed *MinistryToolBox* newsletter reaches more than 85,000 church leaders. As for his own church, its database contains contact information for 40,000-plus visitors, who have available to them multiple weekend services held in diverse venues. Annual church tithes total $27 million, and the church's staff numbers more than 300 full- and part-time workers.

Such numbers are impressive, to say the least. But they actually mean little to Warren, according to recent interviews and sermons he has preached. More important to him than numbers are the people whose lives have been, and are continuing to be, changed by his purpose-driven teachings. In 2004, for example, more than 3000 people accepted Christ as their Savior at Saddleback Church. There also were 2029 baptisms that year. Then, at the 2005 Easter services, 4146 "seekers" made commitments for Jesus Christ after hearing Warren talk to them about God's five purposes for their lives.

But discovering God's purposes for life is not always as easy as just hearing a sermon, especially given the lamentable state of the world and every human being's separation from God. Consider the story of 34-year-old Brian Nichols—a murderer— and 26-year-old Ashley Smith, his hostage for seven hours.

## A Murderer, a Mom, and a Miracle

This story of hope in the midst of hopelessness began in Atlanta, Georgia, starting at 8:00 AM on March 11, 2005, when

Nichols, who was on trial for rape, escaped from authorities while on his way to court.

Before midnight, the desperate man had killed four people. How or why he ended up in a truck parked outside Ashley Smith's apartment, no one knows. But when she returned home from an errand at around two o'clock in the morning on March 12, Nichols was waiting. He got out of his vehicle and approached her before she could enter her apartment, then brandished a gun, warning her, "Don't scream."[4]

"Please don't hurt me," Smith pleaded. "I have a 5-year-old little girl."

The two entered the apartment, where they remained until after dawn. But the situation did not develop in any way that was typical. Smith not only continued begging Nichols to not kill her, but she told him of the murder four years earlier of her husband, who had been stabbed. And she spoke again of her daughter, who was staying elsewhere, telling her captor that "the little girl didn't have a daddy anymore"; and that if she, too, were killed, then her daughter "wouldn't have a mommy either."

Nichols's heart kept softening, until Smith finally asked if she could pass the time by reading her 40-day devotional guide, *The Purpose-Driven Life*. Nichols said yes, even allowing her to read some of it to him. She began, "We serve God by serving others.... In our self-serving culture, with its *me-first* mentality, acting like a servant is not a popular concept. Jesus, however, measured greatness in terms of service, not status."[5]

Nichols stopped her. "Will you read it again?"

She read the passage again, this time going on to another section that, as she reported, "mentioned something about what you thought your purpose in life was."

Miraculously, by 9:00 AM, Nichols had decided to release

Smith. But before she left, he asked, "What do you think I should do?"

"I think you should turn yourself in," she responded.

And that's exactly what he did. After her release, Smith proceeded to call 9-1-1, believing that Nichols just might do the right thing, especially in light of her conversation with him early that morning. He had implied to her that all he really needed in life was a little hope, explaining he felt like he was a dead man.

But she had disagreed. "Do you believe in miracles?" she had asked him. "You're here for a reason. You're here in my apartment for some reason." She added, "You know, your miracle could be that you need to be caught for this. [Maybe] you need to go to prison and you need to share the Word of God with all the prisoners there."

When police finally arrived on the scene, there was no struggle with the killer; no shoot-out; no suicide. Something had changed.

## More Than a Book

Getting people to realize God's purposes (see page 7) is what *The Purpose-Driven Life* is all about. Additionally, the book contains many other standard Christian teachings long held and widely taught throughout Judeo-Christian history:[6]

1. There is a personal God.

2. God created all of us—and as His creations, each of us has a purpose (a reason to live) that is ordained by God (consider Jeremiah's calling as a prophet *before* his birth—see Jeremiah 1:5).

3. Without God everyone is hopelessly lost in sin and ignorant of their true purpose (which according to the

Puritans was to glorify God). Fortunately, Jesus came to die for our sins on the cross. And by accepting His sacrifice by faith we receive not only eternal life, but also purpose (that is to say, our *personal* way of glorifying God).

4. *True* peace, joy, and fulfillment in life are given by God only to those having a "relationship" with Him through Christ. Just being "religious" is not good enough.

5. Since purpose is found only by knowing, loving, and serving God, then life without God is meaningless (see Ecclesiastes 1:2).

According to Rick Warren, then, one's decision to stop living for the "self" and start living for God is pivotal. But this is something that can only be accomplished by accepting Jesus as one's personal Lord and Savior. *There is no other way to find purpose.* Why? Because it is God who has numbered our days for *His* good purposes.[7] As Paul the apostle noted, "We are his workmanship, created in Christ Jesus unto good works, which God hath before ordained that we should walk in them."[8]

Now, thanks to *The Purpose-Driven Life,* millions are embracing this concept. The book has convinced longtime atheists that there is a God. Countless people longing to reconnect with God but embittered by bad religious experiences have returned to their spiritual roots. Many convicts in American prisons have become less violent and turned their hearts to God. And an untold number of those lost in the depths of anguish, confusion, desperation, and hopelessness are finding a reason to live.

In the simplest of terms, Rick Warren's mega-bestseller seems to be helping a lot of people find Jesus and focus on God as the only source of truth. In turn they have begun to live righteous, holy, fulfilling, productive, and meaningful lives as they love and serve God. And just as the Bible promises,[9] they are able to

- remain joyful and at peace in the midst of suffering
- accept their strengths and weaknesses more readily, knowing that God created them in a specific way and for a specific reason—just as a potter fashions a work of clay
- see life, the world, themselves, and others from a biblical perspective
- put God and His desires first in all situations
- appreciate life more fully
- make godly choices rather than sinful choices
- contribute positively to the world

Who could argue with any of that? Surprisingly, a lot of people. But the most vocal critics of *The Purpose-Driven Life* are not atheists or leaders of competing religions—they are Christians, some of whom are quite well-known and influential. Interestingly, many of these individuals are either former cultists or people whose entire ministerial lives are devoted to rooting out the false doctrines of cults, the occult, and world religions. Although zealous and well-meaning, they have leveled a slew of false charges against Warren, decrying his book as a presentation of "New Age" beliefs and a wide assortment of heretical concepts. Even more surprising is how their groundless accusations are now being repeated by a significant number of senior pastors throughout America. Some of these pastors, in fact, have become Warren's harshest detractors. As a result, there now exist a growing number of lay Christians who are not only accepting such criticisms as true but are repeating them to others.

## For What It's Worth

Clearly, the complaints currently being lodged against Warren, his faith, Saddleback Church, and *The Purpose-Driven Life* are serious. He has been called a promoter of "heresy" as well as a dispenser of "poison."[10] Allegations that he advocates false spiritualities abound. In response to these and other accusations I offer *Rick Warren and the Purpose That Drives Him*. I hope to make some long overdue corrections to the inaccurate statements that have been made about Warren and his views.

But I write not just as someone who has been a researcher of religious belief systems for many years. I also write as an insider. Saddleback has been my church since 1995. I worked on its staff as Creative Arts Director from 1998 to 2000. I personally know Rick Warren, his family, and his friends. I have heard him preach hundreds of times. And though I am no longer on staff, I volunteer at the church in various ministries. I live the purpose-driven life, and I see others living it as well.

I was also given unprecedented access to Warren and his personal files, as well as to leaders at Saddleback Church and to internal church documents relating to the issues discussed throughout the following pages. For example, I received transcripts of most, if not all, of the talks Warren has given since 1984! Included in these transcripts were not only the sermons he has preached at Saddleback's weekend services, but also messages he has delivered during Purpose-Driven Church conferences, Leadership Training Seminars, and private church functions. Warren also gave me access to searchable electronic versions of his books, sermon notes, preaching outlines, and staff-only talks.

All of this documentation paints a very different picture of Warren than the one being painted by those seeking to "expose" his so-called heresy, false teachings, and willingness to compromise the Gospel. The documents show that on countless occasions Warren has expressed his absolute dedication to defending the faith, his unwavering commitment to the purity of the historic Christian Gospel, and his love for fellow pastors who might in some way benefit from the knowledge he has gained over the years.

Am I saying that Rick Warren, his book *The Purpose-Driven Life,* and Saddleback Church have no flaws? No. Do I think that every word Warren has ever spoken or written has been done so perfectly? No. Warren, like all of us, is an imperfect sinner saved by God's grace. Every church, likewise, is imperfect because each one is run by imperfect people.

But imperfections do not make someone a heretic, a "false teacher" who is "leading the Church astray," a proponent of "radical departures from historic Christian teachings," or any of the other epithets being applied to Warren. Some critics are implying he is not even a Christian.[11]

In the following pages I will examine such accusations, paying careful attention to Warren's sermons that address the doctrinal areas causing so much controversy. I will also briefly cover his early life, how he started Saddleback Church, and the spiritual roots that place him squarely in the center of mainstream, orthodox Christianity. First, though, I offer an exclusive interview with Warren in which he presents himself, his faith, and his heart. His own words express—once and for all, in the clearest of terms— the truth about Rick Warren and the purpose that drives him.

# Rick Warren
# in His Own Words

I walked into Rick Warren's office around noon on May 4, 2005. It is a medium-sized work space—bright, clean, and modestly furnished with a desk, a few bookshelves, a small sofa, and a couple of chairs.

"Hey, Rick!" I said.

He looked up from his laptop. "Hey, Richard, how ya doing? Come on in."

We shook hands as I took my seat, eager to get down to business. But Warren, being a pastor, seemed more interested in just chatting. "How's your wife?" he asked.

"Oh, fine. She's doing fine. I've been working hard, though, pulling long days."

"Yeah, you look tired, buddy. You look tired."

Rick clowning around at the microphone during a private luncheon for staff and former staff that was held just before Saddleback's Twenty-Fifth Anniversary Celebration service. "I want everyone to eat as much as you can! I bought a lot of food, and I want you all to eat and eat until you can't eat any more!"

Our informal conversation lasted just a few more moments, both of us realizing time was at a premium and our personal friendship had to be set aside in deference to our more official purpose. The interview began.

**RA:** Okay, I've got a question for you: Where did your now-famous Hawaiian shirt and no-socks look for preaching come from? [Warren laughs.] Because I've got pictures of you—

**RW:** Yeah.

**RA:** —preaching at Saddleback, a time long ago, in a suit and tie!

**RW:** [laughs] Well, here's a little-known fact. When I started the church, I started in a three-piece suit, with tie, because I was trying to make myself look a little bit older [laughs]. I was only 25 years old and wanted to have a little *gravitas* [laughs]. But after preaching for many years in hot gymnasiums with no air-conditioning, it started to become a practical matter. At first I began to take off my coat. Then, in the summer, I began to take off my tie. Eventually I went to short-sleeve shirts, then just said, "Folks, it's so hot in here, just wear what's comfortable." And I happen to like bright colors.

**RA:** So that transferred naturally over into the church—a very casual atmosphere?

**RW:** Yeah, there was no strategy behind it [laughs]. Now people look at the shirt and think there's *something* behind it [laughs]. But no, it's nothing. It just happened. In fact, it's gotten so stereotyped that I've actually started wearing other kinds of shirts!

**RA:** Okay, a bit more seriously, what does it feel like to be not only a *New York Times* bestselling author, but also "America's Pastor," which is what you're being called?

**RW:** [pause] Humbling. [pause] Surprising. And it is a stewardship. If God gives you some kind of prominence, then it's not for your own ego. It's definitely to be used for His glory. It's a stewardship of *affluence* and a stewardship of *influence*.

Rick in his pre-Hawaiian-shirt days (about the mid-1980s), when he was trying to make himself look a bit older for the crowds. "I was only 25 years old and I wanted to have a little *gravitas*."

**RA:** Has your life changed?

**RW:** Richard, I've only had two goals for my life. First, I wanted to pastor Saddleback Church for life. I believe in the stability of long-term pastors. I wanted to see a generation grow up, then get married; another generation grow up, then get married. And people would say, "Oh, that's just Pastor Rick, he's been here for 40 years." You need islands of stability that people can depend on. Now, I've watched an entire generation go through preschool, grade school—watched them come to Christ, baptized them, watched them grow up, graduate, then get married.

And that gives me a great thrill as a pastor. I have a pastor's heart and I love my church—just being here.

The other goal was simply to train pastors. I care about pastors, particularly the average pastor of the average church. I dedicated *The Purpose-Driven Church* to bivocational pastors—the guy who's working a 40-hour job and then trying to pastor a small church on the weekend. Those are the guys I care about—not the big megachurch pastors. Those are the kinds of churches I grew up in— little churches.

## Affluence and Influence

**RA:**  How did it all start?

**RW:**  The first ten years of Saddleback was our *local* decade. From '80 to '89 I just wanted to build a model of the healthy church. In the '90s we went *national*—we're blessed to be a blessing; what God has helped us with, we're to help others in. So we started training other pastors. Then, in the twenty-first century, I said, "We're going to go *global.*" There are millions of pastors in third-world countries that have no training at all. These are the guys I care about. They don't have high school, college, much less any seminary training.

**RA:**  But *The Purpose-Driven Life* changed things?

**RW:**  Two years ago, *three* things changed my life: one was the success of the book; one was something that happened in Kay's life; and one was a trip to Africa.

**RA:**  Let's talk about the book's success first.

**RW:** The book brought in millions of dollars—millions and millions of dollars. And it brought in a lot of notoriety.

**RA:** Well, the question is obvious: Where's all of the money going?

**RW:** I began to ask God, "What do You want me to do with the *affluence?* What do You want me to do with the *influence?*" I don't think God gives you money or fame for your ego. It's actually a stewardship: "What do *You* want to do, God, with *Your* money and *Your* platform?" It's not about me. That's the first sentence of the book. I never knew when I wrote the book that I would be tested over and over and over by that first sentence, "It's not about you." So I said, "God, show me what to do with the money and the influence."

**RA:** And?

**RW:** And God gave me 1 Corinthians 9 from the New Testament and Psalm 72 from the Old Testament. Kay and I then made five decisions about the money: 1) We would not change our lifestyle one bit. We didn't buy a bigger house; didn't buy a new car [Warren's car is a four-year-old Ford]. I don't own a vacation home. I don't own a yacht. 2) I stopped taking a salary from the church as of two-and-a-half years ago. 3) I added up all the church had paid me in the last 25 years, and I gave it back. I knew I'd be under the spotlight. And the very next week one of those major secular magazines came and asked me, "What's your salary?"—*first question!* And I go, "Well, actually, I've served my church free for the last 25 years." You know, they always *expect* you to be getting rich off of some megachurch. *And I know every pastor would do the same* *thing if they could.* It's not some holy, spiritual thing I've done. *Every* guy I know would do it for free. 4) We set up three foundations—one for training pastors, one for the P.E.A.C.E. fund, and one for helping those infected with AIDS. And 5) Kay and I became reverse tithers. We now give 90 percent away and live on 10 percent of our income. [I have learned that in 2004 Rick and Kay Warren contributed approximately $13 million to charities.]

**RA:**  What about the *influence* part of it?

**RW:**  God led me to Psalm 72. That is Solomon's prayer for more influence. It sounds like a selfish prayer [for success, influence, fame, blessings, and power]. But then he says, so that the king may care for the widow and orphan, support the oppressed, defend the defenseless, care about the prisoner, help the foreigner, and on and on—it's all the marginalized of society. And God said to me, *The purpose of influence is to speak up for those who have no influence.* That changed my life. I had to repent. I said, "God, I can't think of the last time I thought about widows and orphans. They're not on my agenda. I'm building a big church, in a very affluent area with gated communities." You know, there aren't any homeless people on the streets here.

**RA:**  That's true.

**RW:**  And I said, "I'm sorry, God. How did I miss those 2000 verses on the poor in the Bible? How did I miss that with all my training, doctrine, and education? How did I miss that?"

**RA:**  How does this fit into the AIDS project?

**RW:**  Six months prior to my finding Psalm 72, Kay had read a *Time* magazine article about AIDS in Africa, and there was one line that got her: "Twelve million orphaned by AIDS in Africa." She couldn't imagine twelve million being orphaned by *anything,* much less AIDS. And God said to her, *Are you going to let Me use you? Or, are you going to just go with your own plans?* Her plan was to be a sweet pastor's wife, teach Bible studies, teach "Foundations," raise her kids, and be a homemaker. Then she had a decision: "Am I going to let God break my heart—or not?" And she decided to let Him break it. She shared that with me before I saw Psalm 72, and told me how she was supposed to be a spokesperson for AIDS.

And I supported her. It was not *my* vision, but I supported her. But then I began to catch the burden too. I thought, *I've got to care about this. I can't ignore this. If we don't speak up about AIDS, it'll be like the church that didn't speak up for 300 years about slavery.* What were they thinking? *And a hundred years from today, maybe they'll say, "Shame on them for not caring about the biggest health crisis in history."* So that was the second event.

**RA:**   Okay, so you first had this mega-bestseller that brought in all kinds of affluence and influence. Then, Kay had her experience, which was followed up by God leading you to Psalm 72. What about the third thing that changed your life and ministry—the trip to Africa?

**RW:**   We went to Africa to teach *Purpose-Driven Church* and train about 90,000 pastors, and I went out to a little village and found a guy in a tent church—75 people (25 orphaned by AIDS and 50 adults). And he goes, "I know who you are." I asked, "How do you know who I am?" He said, "I get your sermons every week [on the Internet in the post office]." And he said, "You're the *only* training I've ever had." Then I thought to myself, *I will give the rest of my life to these guys.* But I realized as I began to talk with him that there were other issues besides church training that needed to be taken care of: poverty, illiteracy, business training, education, and health issues.

## The P.E.A.C.E. Plan

**RA:**     This is how you came up with your P.E.A.C.E. Plan?

**RW:**     Yeah. I began to think, *God, You get the most glory when You attack the biggest giants* (like when David takes on Goliath). So I thought, *What are the biggest problems in the world?* And God gave me, that night in Africa, under the skies, these five things—the global Goliaths. First, spiritual emptiness. People are lost. They don't know the name of Jesus Christ. They're lost without Christ. They don't know Jesus saves. They don't know God has a plan and purpose for their lives. They don't know that they're not an accident. Second, we have egocentric leaders, not servant-leaders like Jesus. They don't lay down their lives for the sheep. They think people exist for them. We *cannot* get at these world problems until people start learning servant leadership—to lead like Jesus. Third, poverty. Fourth, disease—and diseases that we have cures for. But they're not eradicated because we don't have the leadership, we don't have the guts to say, "We're going to stop this!" We know the cures: malaria, typhus, yellow fever, waterborne eye diseases, measles, mumps, etc. And AIDS, which we don't have a cure for, but it's 100-percent preventable. Fifth, illiteracy and education. Half the world is functionally illiterate. So I went to Scripture and said, "What's Your plan?"

And God led me to Luke 10, where Jesus sends out the seventy and mentions the man of peace in every village— the man of *peace.*

**RA:** This brings up an interesting point. Neale Donald Walsch—the New Ager—do you know he's got *his* New Age "PEACE Plan?"

**RW:** Oh, no—I didn't know that.

**RA:** You didn't know that?

**RW:** No, uh-uh.

**RA:** Yeah, he has a "PEACE Plan."

**RW:** [laughs]

**RA:** Just happens to be called a "Peace Plan."

**RW:** [laughs again, louder] Well, I'm sure you can find a hundred peace plans.

**RA:** Yeah, some of your critics are connecting your P.E.A.C.E. Plan with his "Peace Plan" and hear you use the word "global," then the idea is—[Warren laughs again]—you know, you are in cahoots with these New Agers to do a "Peace Plan."

**RW:** How funny. Nope, never met him. [My peace plan] is not globalism, it's church-ism. The P.E.A.C.E. Plan is built on local churches—built on the idea that these problems are so big they cannot be solved by anybody except the church. *That's* the P.E.A.C.E. Plan. Nothing else is big enough—no businesses, no education, no governments. The UN isn't big enough. It is only the millions of local churches spread around the world [that are big enough]. You can go into any village without a clinic, or school, or store, or post office [around the world]—but they've got a church. And *that* church can become the center of the community if it is properly trained to do so. Historically, it is the church that has led the way in health care, education, and literacy. Christianity has always led the way.

## A New Reformation

**RA:** Why do you think there's such apprehension [about your P.E.A.C.E. Plan]?

**RW:** Because of the "social gospel." This is a term for liberalism, which means all we care about is feeding bodies, and not saving them. It says, "We don't really need personal salvation anymore, we don't need the atonement, we don't need Jesus' blood. All we need is to redeem the social structures of society and man will automatically get better." It's Marxism in religious form. And it's typical of the Darwinism and Marxism of the late-nineteenth century.

**RA:** This is not what you're advocating?

**RW:** *Not at all!* The church has always cared for the body, mind, and spirit. We do healing, caring, loving. We don't just care for the spirit. We care for people—the poor. Jesus cared for the poor. All the prophets railed against those who weren't caring for the poor.

But Protestantism split into two wings. First, the liberal mainline churches, which are now just sideline churches, they took the social gospel. They simply became excuses for rich people to give to charity. There was no Gospel in it, just "I will soothe my conscience by helping the poor and we will work for social justice." In reaction, fundamentalists, and later evangelicals, said, "We're just going to focus on salvation. You need Jesus, come forward, get saved." But we didn't talk about the needs of people—the sick, the poor, the depressed, and the oppressed.

It's time to bring these back together. I am calling for a return to nineteenth-century evangelicalism. It's more muscle and less mouth. It was the evangelicalism of Charles Spurgeon, who started schools and orphanages all around England *as well as* teaching the Gospel. It is the evangelicalism of William Booth—the Salvation Army—who said, "The whole Gospel, for the whole man, for the whole world."

**RA:** It's James: "I'll show you my faith by my works."

**RW:** It's James. And that's why the "New Reformation" is not about creeds, it's about deeds. It's not about belief, it's about behavior. We figured out the correct beliefs 500 years ago. We've got our doctrinal beliefs. Here's what the Bible says. *Sola Scriptura. Sola Gratia. Sola Fide. Soli Deo Gloria.* But now we need a reformation of behavior. What does the church *do* in the world? Christians are known today only for what they're against. We've had the feet and the hands of the body of Christ amputated and we're just a big mouth. And we're just known for what we're against. Now, I am still against homosexuality. Still against stem-cell research. Still against abortion. But that's not the whole agenda. The world's problems are poverty, disease, and spiritual emptiness. People need Christ. We're not going to back off of all of these *other* things, but they're not all we are.

**RA:** What about the "Emerging Church"? There are a lot of concerns about its high degree of subjectivity, which may lead to relativism. What do you think about that, and how do you see your "purpose-driven" model for life and the church fitting into that?

**RW:** Okay, let me start by telling you what purpose-driven church is *not*. First, it has *nothing* to do with the size of your church. There are little, tiny purpose-driven churches, medium-sized churches, large churches, and mega-churches.

**RA:** Most have about 100 to 200 members, right?

**RW:** Absolutely! The vast majority of purpose-driven churches have 100 people. And it's *not* about denominations. It's not simply a "Baptist" thing. It's *not* about your "target." You may be urban, rural, or suburban. It has nothing to do with location or worship style. Saddleback has started many daughter churches, and not one of them uses our exact worship style. In fact, at Saddleback now, we use eight *different* worship styles. And it is *not* even about being seeker-sensitive. It's not! It's about building a church on God's purposes: worship, fellowship, maturity, service, and evangelism.

**RA:** Health over growth?

**RW:** That's right. But if you don't have a structure to give equal balance to all five, then you're going to emphasize the one that the pastor cares about the most. You might be good at building maturity, but there's no evangelism. You might be good at evangelism, but there's no ministry going on. Or, you might be good at ministry, but there's no fellowship. A lot of churches are great at fellowship, but not so good at the rest. You know, the family-reunion kind of church. It's also *not* about whether you are pretty modern, post-modern, or modern. And age doesn't matter either. And it's not a boomer or a Gen-X model. It's not even an American model. There are more purpose-driven churches *not* in America than in America. It's about structuring on purpose.

## Postmodernism and the "Emerging Church"

**RA:**   And what about the Emerging Church?

**RW:**   Let me talk specifically about what I think is most important—the Emerging Church's preoccupation with postmodernism. Postmodernism has never created anything. It is only destructive. It deconstructs. It cannot build anything, and so it will be dead in a matter of years. It cannot last. It is a fad. But it is so like the church to jump on the bandwagon just as everyone is jumping off. Postmodernism is just a little, dinky, tiny sliver of young to middle-age, college-educated, affluent white people in America.

**RA:**   And relativism?

**RW:**   Well, postmodernism is totally relativistic because they say there are no absolutes. And that's why it is incompatible with Christianity. It's just incompatible. You cannot say that there are no absolutes.

**RA:**   That's interesting, because various postmodernists have been linked to you.

**RW:**   Postmodernism is wimpy. They're going in a different direction [than I am].

**RA:**   But still, your name—

**RW:**   For instance, I debated Brian McLaren, [author of *The Church on the Other Side* and *A New Kind of Christian*] in *Christianity Today* over *The Passion*. I said, "Wait a minute—Jesus said, 'If I be lifted up I will draw all men unto me.' You're telling me that the Gospel put in visual is not a good evangelism tool? How can you say that?"

**RA:** And also Ken Blanchard, who is not postmodern, but he does seem to be somewhat pluralistic.

**RW:** No. Blanchard's not a postmodernist. He's just not a deep Christian.

**RA:** Well, that's the question everyone has. Because he wrote an endorsement for Deepak Chopra's *The Seven Spiritual Laws of Success*—and forewords to other books by New Agers and Buddhists.

**RW:** Here's the thing—he doesn't even get it all yet. In fact, I explained the diamond [see pages 58–61] to him and I said, "You know what, Ken, you stole second base. You started in ministry *before* you got to maturity." And he said, "You're right." He admits it. He says, "All of a sudden I'm out there talking because I was so well-known." And he was trying; he's *trying* do something for the Lord. He's just...[pause]

I'll give you an example. He gives me that book *The Celestine Prophecy,* and he says, "Rick, I don't know what to think of this. What do you think about it?" Well, I hadn't even seen it because I hadn't heard about it. But I read it real quick—pure junk. Wrote a summary of it and said, "Ken, don't ever tell anybody to endorse this book. Don't ever give it to anybody because it's New Age and here are the ten things wrong with it." And he said, "Oh, thank you!" He just needs to be taken aside and instructed in the ways of the Lord.

**RA:** These are the questions a lot of people are asking.

**RW:** Well, I do know Ken Blanchard. But we're not close

friends—no closer friends than half-a-dozen other celebrities I know.[1]

**RA:** Have you *hired* him?

**RW:** No. [surprised look]

**RA:** That's what George Mair's book *[A Life of Purpose]* says.

**RW:** No, no, I never hired him. [sounds of exasperation]

**RA:** The unauthorized biography—

**RW:** [laughs] George Mair *says* that Norman Vincent Peale is my model.

**RA:** And [Robert] Schuller is your mentor!

**RW:** And Schuller is my mentor!

**RA:** Okay, wait. *Is* Schuller your mentor?

**RW:** *No!* Never has been, never would be!

## Orthodox on Purpose

**RA:** Well, let me just ask you some yes-and-no questions.

**RW:** Okay. Sure.

**RA:** Do you advocate watering down the Gospel to cater to seekers?

**RW:** Absolutely not! Let me tell you what I *do* believe. The *message* must never change, but the *methods* must change. If you change the message, you are a heretic. Here's a direct quote [moves toward microphone and speaks loudly]: "YOU ARE A HERETIC IF YOU CHANGE THE MESSAGE. THE BIBLE SAYS IN JUDE, IT IS THE FAITH 'ONCE FOR ALL DELIVERED TO THE SAINTS.' IT *CANNOT* BE TAMPERED WITH." At the same time, however, I also believe that if you continue to share it in an outdated mode, for instance, like a preaching style that was effective a hundred years ago, *you* are actually making the message watered down because people can't hear it.

**RA:** When you talk a lot about being "global" and reaching out to the world, are you talking about any kind of spiritual globalism—a New Spirituality—wherein all religious divisions are removed?

**RW:** Not at all. It is simply a call for local churches to *be* the church in all of its expressions. I believe the twenty-first century is the era of the local church. And it should be the goal of parachurches to support the churches, not vice versa, because Jesus said, "I will build my church."

**RA:** So there is, in your opinion, *no way* to be saved outside of a personal faith in the historic, orthodox Jesus of the Bible.

**RW:** Absolutely not. John 14:6. Very clear. I'm betting my life on John 14:6.

**RA:** So you do not endorse or adhere to Robert Schuller's teachings on things like sin, salvation, and pluralism?

**RW:** Absolutely not! Not only do I not endorse him—*he's wrong!* He's just flat-out wrong.

**RA:** Here's an off question: Do you kick people out of Saddleback for not signing the church membership covenant?

**RW:** Well, you can't *join* without the covenant. That's true.

**RA:** But you don't remove people for not signing?

**RW:** No, no, no.

**RA:**   Why do you have covenants? Some people say they're cultic.

**RW:**   Is the Nicene Creed cultic? Are the different creeds cultic? No. They're simply affirmations of faith. Any apologist should understand that it is important to clarify up front what you believe. So we ask people to clarify that they agree with our beliefs before joining. And I would think that apologists would support that, rather than be offended by it. If you can join a church without having to affirm any kind of creed or a covenant, then you can have unbelievers as members in your church.

## Final Perspective

**RA:**   Shifting gears now, what's the most rewarding aspect of all that has happened to you?

**RW:**   I now know that God made the book successful to create a platform, to mobilize the church, for a new reformation. That it has been a platform for great renewal—tens of thousands of churches have been renewed. That is exciting to me: changed lives.

**RA:**   So where do you see Saddleback in 25 years, in maybe 2030? How big will Saddleback be? 100,000 members? A different kind of church?

**RW:**   Well, the future growth of Saddleback is in the hands of the Lord. We will never stop reaching out as long as there is one person who doesn't know Christ. Because what motivates us is not size. Not who's in, but who's still out. You may have 99 in the fold, but if there's one still out, you are *commanded* to keep going. So what will

Saddleback's *size* be in 25 years? I don't know. What will Saddleback be *doing* in 25 years? Still reaching out.

And we will be reaching out through planting other churches and training other churches. We've never been about building the biggest church. We've been more about mobilizing. You don't judge a church by its seating capacity, but by its sending capacity. Don't compare churches. But if you are going to compare churches, don't compare attendance. What I would ask you to compare are the things that matter. How many of them are tithers? How many of them have a quiet time? How many have been on a mission? How many are serving in a ministry? Habits that show the development of their life. How many of them have shared their faith with someone else? *Forget attendance*—and look at God's purposes.

**RA:**    Okay, here's your parting shot. If someone—critic, fan, unbeliever, Christian, anyone—was to pick up this book, and read just this last part of the interview, what is the one thing you would want to say to them?

**RW:**    I would say, "Jesus is the answer for the world today, above Him there's no other, Jesus is the Way." It's *all* about God. It's *not* about us. You were made *by* God and you were made *for* God. And until you understand that, life will not make sense. Really, it's all about God. And the myth that those "seeker" churches, that they're selling out—well, the truth is that *every* church caters to somebody. If you don't believe that, next week change your order of service, change your music, change your sermon—and you'll know exactly who you're catering to.

**RA:**    That brings up "church splits." There have been complaints about "everybody" over 65 years old in a church being "kicked out" because of Rick Warren. Or things like "Everybody who didn't go along with the 'Rick Warren' program was ousted from the church." What do you say to that?

**RW:** A lot of people take a good message and pervert it. That's been done with every single message in the last 2000 years. Anybody can be misquoted; anybody can be misused. There are a lot of things done in the name of "purpose-driven" that I would publicly disavow. I feel *no* compulsion to defend every stupid mistake that every pastor has made in the name of "purpose-driven."

**RA:** Rick, what one mistake have you made in the years past, as you look back?

**RW:** [pause] My mistake would be [pause] not trusting God even more. It would be hell to know what God could have done in my life if I had been even more committed—more available, more usable, more humble, more pure. To look back and hear God say, *Yeah, I did that, but I could have done this if you had been even more usable* [pause]. That would be...that would be, really, a difficult thing to see. But the greatest joy is that God uses us in spite of ourselves. We're trophies of grace. We don't deserve it. Nobody's more surprised than I am. I'm along for the ride. And it isn't about me. It *is* all about God.

# CHAPTER I

# Here I Am, Lord

*I'll do the best I can, with what I have,*
*for Jesus Christ today.*

JIMMY WARREN (1919–1999),
RICK WARREN'S FATHER

By the time Rick Warren was born in 1954,[1] his parents—Jimmy and Dorothy (known as "Dot")—had been serving the Lord for many years. Jimmy had the "gift of giving." Dot had the "gift of hospitality." And their union made for a remarkable team that manifested God's love in the most basic of all Christian ways: service to others.

They met at church in 1943, dated for two months, and got married at the close of a three-week engagement that began on Valentine's Day. Then, after only two months of marriage, Jimmy left his bride for the war in the South Pacific. Dot recalled, "When he returned two years later we were total strangers, but we were married to each other."

War was only the first of many life twists that would challenge the couple's faith. For example, soon after God called Jimmy into full-time church work, they hit a major financial crisis—despite the "whopping salary" of $5 a week that Jimmy was earning as pastor of one of his first churches. But the couple never stopped trusting God. As Dot would later say, "God has miraculously, and I mean miraculously, paid our bills and met our needs when we had no idea where the money would come from."

## Faith of Our Fathers

To say that the Warrens had an open-door policy at their home would be an understatement. There was a constant parade of church folk (known and unknown) traipsing in and out—not just to visit, but also to enjoy Dot's home-cooked meals. Guests would arrive at some point during the day, remain for dinner, then just stay. "Every night somebody was coming," Rick Warren once told his congregation. "I'd wake up in the morning and wonder who was going to be there for breakfast."

The number of meals Dot served to others would eventually total well into the thousands. This, despite the fact the family was quite poor. To compensate for their monetary shortfall, Jimmy always maintained a lush fruit and vegetable garden. He planted all kinds of trees, flowers, and grass. He was happiest when working with his hands—the quintessential "'hands-on' kind of guy."

Jimmy loved planting and building, especially churches. His carpentry skills proved invaluable in constructing sanctuaries, missionary homes, and Sunday schools. He would ultimately help start some 150 churches worldwide—including one in his own barn, using old theater seats. In 1999, Rick fondly remembered this particular project, explaining, "I grew up watching both Mom and Dad create something out of nothing."

Such acts of service would profoundly affect Rick's own vision, with regard to his belief that one of the five main purposes of a Christian is to serve. From many of his sermons it is obvious that his father had a particularly profound affect on him. As he once said, "The older I get, the more I see how much like my dad I really am."

This is strikingly evident in Warren's sermons, which are punctuated by nuggets of wisdom from Jimmy, a simple country preacher. Consider these godly gems:

- "If you don't hit oil after 20 minutes, stop boring."

- "Aim for the moon and hit the fence post. And watch God raise the sights of the people."

- "Your *first* ministry is never your *greatest* ministry. It is always preparation for what God will eventually do through you."

Two-year-old Rick Warren gone fishin' with his dad, Jimmy, who let him steer the outboard. "If I could summarize my dad's life, I'd say: 'A hammer, and a Bible, and a fishing pole.'" Rick also happens to be a fourth generation preacher. Jimmy was the son of a lay pastor. And Rick's great-grandfather was "led to Christ in Charles Spurgeon's church, went to Spurgeon's college and was sent by Spurgeon to America as a circuit rider [preacher]." Such a lineage has undoubtedly inspired Warren. Even more critical, however, were those times he describes as his having been led by the Spirit of God.

## Just a Kid

Although Warren grew up in a very loving home under the care of godly parents, he also grew up as a pastor's kid—a difficult role, to be sure. He attended Sunday school on Sunday morning, Sunday church on Sunday morning, Training Union on Sunday night (as well as Sunday-night service), and a midweek Bible

Proud parents Jimmy and Dot with their son Rick shortly after he married Kay.

study. Add to all of these meetings his obligatory "quiet times" during the week and, as he once remarked, he was supposed to get "eleven new truths into his life every seven days."

The last thing on his young mind was leading a church. He had other interests, like politics and music. In fact, he wanted to be a guitar-playing rock star! If anyone would have told him as a teenager that in less than 20 years he would be pastoring one of America's largest churches, he would have told them, "You're crazy!" He had "no intention of ever being a pastor!"

But everything started going in a different direction around 1970, just before his junior year in high school. Rick was working as a lifeguard at a Christian summer camp, where he saw other kids living how he wanted to live—in service to God. He prayed, *God, if you're really alive, I want to know You*. Perhaps even more important than this moment, however, was a special sermon he heard preached the same year. It essentially became his own life message. He later recalled the pastor's words:

> He said something like this, "What are you going to do with your life? Are you going to make it count or are you just going to waste it? You'll never be happy until you do with your life *what God made you to do*. And until you be what God made you to be." Bam! That was right on the forehead to me! It got my attention and it was a turning point in my life.

Warren was never the same. He changed the course of his life and began thinking that maybe he was supposed to be a pastor—

not a rock star. He first gave evangelism a shot by preaching to the kids back at school, eventually starting a Christian club, and going so far as to sponsor Christian music concerts. He even "gave out New Testaments, produced a Christian musical, and published an underground Christian newspaper." He also started listening more intently to how others preached. As he listened he found himself writing three letters in his Bible's margins—"YBH" ("Yes, But How?"):

> "We need to be godly men!" Yes, but how? "We need to have strong families!" Yes, but how? "We need to be filled with the Spirit!" Yes, but how? "We need to be strong witnesses!" Yes, but how?

What Warren found lacking in the messages he heard would eventually contribute to his coming up with a clearer way of spreading the Gospel— a way he thought would help people better understand both the eternal *and* temporal benefits of knowing, loving, and serving Jesus. The seeds of his purpose-driven life had been planted.

Sixteen-year-old Rick at a youth conference with a friend in about 1970 or 1971, wearing the suede leather jacket he "bargained" for in Mexico.

## Like Father, Like Son

By the time Warren graduated from high school in early 1972, it was clear God was doing an extraordinary thing in his life. Church leaders in California responded by inviting him to speak at various West Coast gatherings. Within two years he would do "over 120 revivals and crusades." His honorariums actually paid for most of his education at California Baptist University (in Riverside).

Nothing was more important to him than growing in his knowledge of God and discovering the best ways to tell people about Jesus. In 1973, for example, he and a friend drove 350 miles just to hear the great Baptist preacher W.A. Criswell (1909–2002) speak in San Francisco. At that time, Criswell was pastoring the largest Baptist church in the world (First Baptist Church of Dallas, Texas).

Warren, who at the time was only 19 years old, would later explain, "For me, as a young Southern Baptist, the opportunity to hear Criswell in person was the equivalent of a Catholic getting to hear the Pope." He still views Criswell as "the greatest American pastor of the twentieth century." Criswell was "a powerful preacher and leader," "an organizational genius," and "incredibly innovative," to use Warren's own words.

If anyone can be credited with being his spiritual mentor and model, it would be this stalwart of Christianity. In fact, it was at the San Francisco event that God confirmed Warren's calling. He still remembers the interaction—Criswell "looked at me with kind, loving eyes and said, quite emphatically, 'Young man, I feel led to lay hands on you and pray for you!'" Criswell then asked God to bless him. "That holy experience confirmed in my heart that God had called me to pastor a local church," Warren recalled. The die had been cast. He was destined to be a church pastor.

Rick and Kay in 1975, the year they got married.

Warren's uplifting encounter with Criswell would always remain a spiritual marker in his life. But many equally significant milestones would quickly begin to come into view as time passed. Even before meeting Criswell, Warren was already attending California

Baptist University, a place where he gained some of his most valuable theological training. It was there, too, that he eventually met Kay Lewis, the love of his life, whom he would marry in 1975—the same year he was ordained. Then, after graduating together in 1977, the two aspiring missionaries would move to Fort Worth, Texas, so Rick could attend Southwestern Theological Seminary.

Graduating from California Baptist University in 1977— a joyous event.

The doctorate Warren earned by the end of 1979 at Southwestern would officially mark his attainment to an extremely important foundation of biblical knowledge, one especially critical to his capacity as the founder of a new church. His education also would contribute in no small measure to the various books that lay in his future: *Personal Bible Study Methods* (1981); *The Purpose-Driven Church* (1995); *Power to Change Your Life* (1998); *Answers to Life's Most Difficult Questions* (1999); and *The Purpose-Driven Life* (2002). And of course, Warren would not only become a bestselling author, but would also end up pastoring one of America's largest churches.

Back in early 1979, however, neither Rick nor Kay could see any of these blessings. But all of that began changing by December of that very same year, as Rick was finishing up his final classes in seminary. He and Kay were about to make one of their biggest leaps of faith—all for God's glory. Saddleback Church was about to be born.

Rick and Kay in 1979, about four years after they got married.

# CHAPTER 2

# Driven by Purpose— Directed by God

*To know God, this is eternal life; this is the purpose for which we are and were created.*

A.W. TOZER (1897–1963),
AMERICAN PASTOR, TEACHER, AUTHOR

Even before graduating from seminary, Warren had shown an interest in how churches worked. He also was saddened by the number of unbelievers unwilling to give church a try. So in order to satisfy his curiosity about these matters (and to complement his studies), he wrote to the 100 largest churches in America, asking them various questions to find out 1) what made churches grow and 2) what made churches healthy.

One common denominator emerged: "In almost all of the very largest churches in America, the pastor has been there 20 years or longer."[1] Warren prayed, "God, I'm willing to go any place in the world, if you'll just give me the privilege of investing my entire life in one location. I don't care where you put me." And true to his resolve, he would turn down an offer to pastor a very large church in Dallas, believing that God wanted him to "take a small church and grow with the church." But where to go?

To answer this question, Rick and Kay hung a map of the world on the wall of their home. For months they prayed. Finally, by the summer of 1979 they had zeroed in on Seattle, San Francisco, Orange County in California, and San Diego—the most unchurched places in America. Warren then discovered that from 1970 to 1980, Orange County's Saddleback Valley had been "the fast-growing area in one of the fast-growing counties in the United States." God, it seemed, was starting to make His will clear.

Warren decided to write to Herman Wooten, the area super-intendent for Southern Baptist churches in Orange County, though he had never met him:

> Dear Mr. Wooten,
>
> I'm thinking about coming to the Saddleback Valley to start a church. I'm not asking for any money. I'm not asking for your support. I just want to know what you think about the area. Does it need churches?

What Warren did not know was that Wooten had already heard about him through other channels and had simultaneously written his own letter:

> Dear Mr. Warren,
>
> I understand you're thinking about starting a new church. Have you ever considered California? Have you ever considered starting a church in the Saddle-back Valley?

The letters crossed in the mail! So Warren flew out to Orange County to check things out. He "prayed, visited with people, talked to realtors and county people." Then, Kay flew out to join him. When they went up on a hill to pray, they felt "a very strong sense" that God was saying, *You are to move to the Saddleback Valley and start a church and spend your entire life building that one church.* They returned to Texas, still unsure, but willing to do whatever God wanted them to do. They asked Him to "either open

The whole family during Christmas 1979, only a week before Rick, Kay, and little Amy left for California. From left to right: Tom Holladay, who would become Rick's associate pastor; Tom's wife, Chaundel (Rick's kid sister); Jimmy, Amy, Kay, Dot, Rick, and his older brother, Jim.

or close the door on Saddleback Valley." A few months later, He opened it.

## California or Bust

Here is where the real story of Saddleback Church begins—in December 1979, the same month Rick graduated from seminary. Rick and Kay, along with their four-month-old daughter, Amy, "packed up all their belongings in a U-Haul truck to begin the journey of a lifetime: a 1500-mile trip to Orange County, California." (The Warrens would eventually have two more children, Josh and Matthew.) Rick and Kay were going to start a church, despite a few minor problems: They had no members, no money, and no building. They also did not know a single soul in the Saddleback Valley.

The three road-weary travelers hit Orange County around 4 PM on January 2, 1980—"nearly penniless." They did not even have a decent supply of money for food, having spent their last thousand dollars to rent the U-Haul they were driving. To make matters worse, they arrived during rush hour. This was terrifying for a country boy like Warren, who had grown up in a town of less than 500 residents (Redwood Valley, California).

There were cars everywhere and thousands of homes dotting the landscape. Rick thought, *God, You've got the wrong guy. What in the world am I doing? I must have missed Your will here. What am I doing?* Then, in the midst of trying to negotiate the vehicular snarls of the I-5 freeway, he felt an odd prompting to just pull off at the approaching exit and stop in at the very first real-estate office to be found. He did so, and he found on duty that day real-estate agent Don Dale.

"I'm here to start a church and I need a place to live," Warren told him. "And we don't have enough money to rent an apartment."

Dale laughed. "Okay. Let's see what we can do."

Somehow, within a couple of hours, the agent was able to find his broke clients a cheap condominium. And the first month would be free! So they took it. Then Rick asked, "Hey, Don, do you go to church anywhere?"

"No."

Warren smiled. "Ah! You're my first member." And sure enough, on January 16, 1980, within the walls of that condo, the very first attendees of Saddleback Valley Community Church met to hear Warren preach. He delivered a message entitled "Faith." Present were Rick, Kay, Amy, Don, Don's wife and daughter, and one other person.

But Warren still had no money. Three weeks after their first meeting, though, the phone rang. "I'm Bill Grady," said the voice on the other end of the line. "We've never met before, but I'm a pastor of a little church in Fullerton. I understand you're starting a new church. What is your financial support?"

"Uh...we don't have any," Warren answered.

Pastor Grady said, "Well, I feel led to pay your rent the first two months."

In 1987, Warren reflected on this event, saying: "God's plan was, *Move! And I will miraculously provide.* I wouldn't give up the lessons I learned the first six months of this church for anything!"

## A Church for the Unchurched

Warren's plan was to attract sheep who had wandered away from the Shepherd, not those who were already in a church. This was the impetus behind one of his most controversial moves: a survey of non-Christians. He thought, *If we're going to reach people who've never been to church, I'd better go out and talk to them and find out what kind of church would interest them—would get their attention.*

So between January and Easter (the date he had slated for his first public service), he spent 12 weeks going door-to-door, canvassing about 2000 homes. If he met a Christian, he thanked them, encouraged them, and went on his way. But when he met someone who did not regularly attend a church, he asked them four questions:

- "Why do you think most people don't attend church?"

- "If you were looking for a church, what things would you look for?"

- "What advice would you give to me as the pastor of a new church that really wants to be of benefit to the community?"

- "How could I, as a pastor, help you?"

Four interesting things were uncovered—and *none* of them had anything to do with changing the substance of the Gospel. First, non-Christians found sermons intolerably boring and totally irrelevant. Second, non-Christians apparently were not being received in a very friendly manner at churches. Moreover, they were habitually being targeted as visitors, when all they wanted to do was blend into the crowd and watch—get their feet wet, so to speak, "without being put on the spot." Third, unbelievers said they heard way too much of an emphasis on money at church, which turned them off. Fourth, and most enlightening, were complaints about the lack of good child care.

So Warren decided to structure his church with the needs of potential members in mind. More importantly, he completely changed his preaching style in an effort to meet the people where they were. He trashed every message he had ever preached (except two) and started from scratch, fashioning the content and delivery of his sermons in a way that would "make sense" to people in the Saddleback Valley.

At a much more personal level, Warren also had to prepare himself for the physical stress he knew would be placed on him because of a brain disorder he continues to battle to this day. It affects him every time he preaches. He was born with a brain-chemistry malady that makes public speaking excruciatingly painful—a genetic problem very resistant to medication. He explains:

My brain overreacts to adrenaline….Throughout child-hood, anytime adrenaline would hit my system, I would faint. Just fall over backwards and pass out. Black out on the spot! All the way through high school,

I took medication for epilepsy (not because I'm an epileptic but for this disorder).

And I still get severe reactions to adrenaline. First I get very dizzy. My vision blurs and then it blacks out. Sometimes I get headaches—severe headaches. Sometimes severe hot flashes. Any of you who have ever seen me speak have seen me wipe my face. But the most common reaction is an absolute sense of irrational panic. Absolute irrational panic! The only way I can explain it is kind of like if you were to fall off the Empire State Building and you're holding on with one finger looking down...

You have absolutely no idea how bad I feel every time I speak. Every single time....I start getting all these things. My head explodes. Blurry vision. Sometimes I'm speaking and I cannot even see the audience. I can't even see them. These symptoms usually last until about 15 to 20 minutes into the message, where I've expended enough adrenaline that my body kind of goes back into normal. So the first part of any message is excruciatingly painful.

But neither physical suffering nor planning difficulties were going to stop Warren from doing what he knew God was calling him to do—build a church.

## It's All in the Details

At this point it is crucial to mention something that is often overlooked by Warren's many critics: In taking his survey and adjusting the church services according to its results, he did not alter the Gospel in any way to accommodate unbelievers. His goal was to uncover a way by which he could move people from where they were (unsaved) to where he wanted them to be (saved). His survey was designed to find out why Orange County residents were so unwilling to go to church—a place where they could hear those truths that could take them to where they all *definitely* needed to be.

Based on the information gathered, he drafted an open letter to the community, beginning, "Dear neighbor—at last a new church for those who have given up on traditional church services." Then, he listed the four main reasons people didn't go to church, adding, "But if you think church ought to be enjoyable, come give us a try."

Over the next several weeks, Warren and his congregation of fewer than ten "hand-addressed and stamped 15,000 letters that went out to the community, inviting them to church!" Their hope and prayer was to get at least 150 people to attend on Easter (April 6), at a service to be held in the performing arts theater of Laguna Hills High School.

But not only did 60 people arrive at the March 30 "practice" service on Palm Sunday (five of whom accepted Christ as their Savior)—on Easter, 205 people showed up! The 26-year-old Warren shared his dream for the church:

- "It is a dream of a place where the hurting, the depressed, the frustrated, and the confused can find life, acceptance, help, hope, forgiveness, guidance, and encouragement."

- "It is a dream of sharing the Good News of Jesus Christ with the hundreds of thousands of residents in south Orange County."

- "It is a dream of welcoming 20,000 members into the fellowship of our church family—loving, learning, laughing, and living in harmony together."

- "It is a dream of developing people to spiritual maturity through Bible studies, small groups, seminars, retreats, and a Bible School."

- "It is a dream of equipping every believer for a significant ministry by helping them discover the gifts and talents God gave them."

- "It is a dream of sending out hundreds of missionaries and church workers all around the world and empowering every member for a personal life mission in the world."

But it was like preaching to a Kiwanis or Rotary Club. They were mostly unbelievers! No one had a Bible or knew any hymns. And at the end of the service, when Warren said, "Let's pray," everyone just looked at each other, not knowing what to do. And as he was about to give the typical "Come to the front" altar call, he noticed a big problem:

All the chairs were glued together and there was no aisle in this building. It was in a theater. And to get out you'd have to go, "Excuse me, excuse me, excuse me..." past about 50 people, walk out around and then walk down to the front. [And] there was no place to go but an orchestra pit. So, what am I going to say—"I'm going to ask thousands of you to come down right now and jump in the pit"? My honest reaction was,

"Oh, God—how can anybody get saved? There's no place to come forward to."

Rick, Kay, and Amy outside their condo (top right) in late 1980, soon after Saddleback had been founded. Some of Saddleback's first members (top left) addressing and hand-stamping Warren's letter to the community about his first Easter service. Warren preaching in his church when it was in Laguna Hills High School theater (left). "Oh, God—how can anybody get saved? There's no place to come forward to."

Such obstacles, although humorous in hindsight, were serious at the time, and they forced Warren to develop a strategy for meeting the many needs of his attendees: spiritual, emotional, and logistical. The altar call, for instance, was first replaced by an invitation to join a counselor in a "Counseling Room." But this smacked of a scary psychiatric ward, as Warren joked in 1997. The unchurched would think, *I trust Rick, but what's going on in* there *I don't know,* and they'd walk out and keep walking."

The "Counseling Room" was eventually replaced by a "Decision Card."

More changes were adopted, and five years into Saddleback's history it was evident that Warren's dream was becoming a reality. At the church's April 7, 1985, Easter services there were 2500 attendees in the Trabuco Hills High School *gymnasium*. Not until 1991, however, did the Saddleback family have the groundbreaking ceremony for the site of their new home. Even so, it was not until 1996 that the main worship center opened.

## The Old Way or No Way

Throughout the early to mid-1980s, when Warren was starting his church, he was already being seen by many individuals as rather controversial because of his nontraditional approach to doing church. Nevertheless, he did get financial support from at least five churches, and he received accolades from *California Southern Baptist* and *Mission USA* magazines. Still, traditionalists uncomfortable with Warren's style labeled him a "liberal" (despite his theological conservatism). Many pastors would not even associate with him. One exception was W.A. Criswell, who, Warren recalls, "understood that while the message of Christ never changes, the methods we use *must* change with every generation."

Criswell comprehended what Warren had come to know: The resilience and power of preaching rests *not* in someone's style of dress or speech, but in the heart of the Gospel message—the life, death, and resurrection of Jesus. Like any good preacher, Warren offers the answer (Jesus) to everyone's problem (sin). That has always been Rick Warren's message. *He has never compromised the essential truths of Christianity.*

He has, however, revamped the traditional ways of organizing and running a church and has radically shifted the *emphasis* of his sermons and writings away from what traditional preachers have always emphasized. In doing so he has made the Gospel more relevant to contemporary people's lives and experiences. This is evident in Saddleback Church's phenomenal growth since 1980.

Today, Saddleback's 100-plus-acre property—complete with worship centers, office facilities, education buildings, and sprawling parking lots—is the spiritual haven to the congregation of the more than 20,000 who go to services there on a typical weekend. But it has come at no small cost. Warren has been "ruthlessly criticized" for many years by traditionalists who refused to accept his way of doing church as legitimate.

Exactly what is Warren's way of doing church? This aspect of his ministry will be the focus of chapter 3.

# CHAPTER 3

# Seekers and Saints

*Saddleback is not a story of numbers.*
*It's the story of individual lives changed one at a time.*
*Every number represents a real person*
*transformed by the power of Jesus Christ.*

RICK WARREN (MAY 3, 2000),
INTERVIEW, *BAPTIST PRESS*

Transforming lives—not just imparting information—is Rick Warren's goal and the purpose of *The Purpose-Driven Life*. This is the same goal so evident in the teachings of Jesus Christ, the greatest preacher who ever lived. His approach was 100-percent life application (or rather, 100-percent life-*changing*). "My model is not anything but following Jesus," Warren explains. "My goal when I preach is *not* to inform; it is to transform."[1]

According to Warren, anyone not offering "life application" sermons is "not preaching the gospel in its fullness."[2] In other words, the Gospel (the life, death, and resurrection of Christ) must always be presented in a relevant way. This is what he considers addressing a person's "felt needs":

> Application is not something that you tack on to the
> end of the message. It *is* the message!...If you haven't

*applied* it you have not preached. You may have given a Bible *lecture*....But you have not preached. Application is the message if you're preaching according to the purpose of God, the purpose of the Bible, and the purpose of preaching—to change lives and to make people like Christ.

This is not to say that the *substance* of the Gospel must be altered. The application of it, however, must change because society changes. Likewise, the language used long ago to preach and sing of the Gospel's great doctrinal truths is not only obscure, but virtually meaningless to twenty-first-century listeners. Consider the hymn "Jesus, Saviour, Pilot Me"—does this mean that Christ flies a plane? What about "There Is a Fountain Filled with Blood!"? To most unbelievers this sounds more like a Stephen King novel than a precious doctrine of the faith.

As Warren has said, "You can't preach Calvin's sermons, because you don't have Calvin's audience." But he adds, "The message must never change. It is the faith *once for all delivered to the saints*' [Jude 3]. We do not have a right to change the message." This is important. Warren has no interest in altering the Gospel of salvation (1 Corinthians 15:1-5). All he wants to do is present it in a way that makes sense to today's unbelievers.

His preaching might be best compared to modern medicine's "smart" drug delivery devices, which target cancer cells for destruction while leaving good cells undamaged. The lifesaving drugs are attached to molecules injected into the body. They kill the cancer more effectively but are better tolerated by the body than radiation or untargeted chemotherapy. The end result is the same—healing.

The disease that Warren wants to treat is that cancer of the soul known as sin—a festering tumor of self-centeredness, spiritual blindness, alienation from God, and the desire for anything but God. His lifesaving drug is the Gospel (the life, death, and resurrection of Jesus for our sins). And the molecules he uses to deliver his "drug" are the *benefits* of the Good News: hope, joy, peace, love, contentment, and of course, purpose.*

## Warren on Salvation

Warren's key to living a meaningful life is not some magic formula for health and happiness. It is the application of God's Word to a person's life for God's glory,[3] which is something that can only be done by accepting Jesus as personal Savior and Lord:

- "[Jesus] died on the cross to pay for my sins and He says, 'If you'll accept Me, you can come into heaven.'"

- "You don't seek God; He seeks you."

- "The difference between religion and Jesus Christ and what He said is this: 'It's nothing you do. It's already been done....I've paid the price.' That's why Jesus, with His arms outstretched on the cross, said, 'It is accomplished. It is finished....All you need to do is trust Me.'"[4]

Only by faith in Christ can anyone enter into God's family—and even *that* is by grace alone through faith alone. This is what leads to a purpose-driven life—also known as a meaningful existence. Everything is changed (2 Corinthians 5:17). As Warren puts it, "You can begin to experience real life here on earth right now."[5] The born-again experience results in a radically altered

---

* See pages 62–63, 70–71, 73.

way of seeing life and living it. Everything is about glorifying God. And "real life" does not mean feeling better about the sinful "self," figuring out how to get what the sinful "self" wants, or accepting the sinful "self" as good. Such self-help nonsense is what the world promises via techniques Warren condemns as empty: "pop psychology," "success motivation," and "inspirational stories."[6]

Similarly, he has denounced anything in the church that is not Christ-centered—for example, social/community "gimmicks" to spur growth, a toleration for sin, and most especially, a watered-down Gospel message that might suggest an "all roads lead to God" view of religion. His entire method for building churches, in fact, is based firmly on various New Testament passages relating to God's people.

## Doing Church

*The Purpose-Driven Church* (1995), it must first be pointed out, is not a book about church growth. It stresses church *"health,"* which Warren believes will naturally produce growth. To illustrate his model for health, he uses a baseball diamond around which church members are to be ushered. It is "a simple process for moving people from unchurched and uncommitted to mature believers who fulfill their ministry in the church and their life mission in the world."[7]

*First Base* corresponds to "C.L.A.S.S. 101" (Discovering Church *Membership*), which "covers salvation, baptism and communion, along with the purposes, targets, structure and affiliations" of the church.

*Second Base* corresponds to "C.L.A.S.S. 201" (Discovering Spiritual *Maturity*), which "focuses on the four basic habits every

Christian needs to grow to spiritual maturity: time in God's Word, prayer, tithing and fellowship."

*Third Base* corresponds to "C.L.A.S.S. 301" (Discovering My *Ministry*), which seeks to help people discover their "unique S.H.A.P.E. for ministry" (in other words, "developing and using their God-given gifts and abilities in serving God and others"). This reflects Saddleback's view that "every member is a minister."[8] ("S.H.A.P.E." is an acronym for how God made us, equipped us, and gifted us for serving Him. It stands for **S**piritual gifts, **H**eart, **A**bilities, **P**ersonality, and **E**xperiences.)

*Home Plate* corresponds to "C.L.A.S.S. 401" (Discovering My Life's *Mission*), which equips people to share their faith with unbelievers. This CLASS is paramount because it relates directly to the Great Commission (Matthew 28:19).

Finally, there is the *Pitcher's Mound,* which is Magnification (or *Worship*). It basically ties together the other bases because everything we do (membership, maturity, ministry, and mission) should be done in worship of God. These stops on the baseball diamond reflect what Warren sees as God's five purposes for the church as delineated by the Bible. They are derived from five commands God has given Christians:

1. Love God with all of your heart (that is to say, worship Him in spirit and in truth—*magnify* Him).

2. Love others "as thyself " and show it through serving God with the gifts and talents He has given you (in other words, *ministry*).

3. Go out into the world and make disciples (also known as evangelism, which is the *mission* of every Christian).

4. Baptize new believers (an act of obedience to God that is often associated with church *membership*).

5. Teach the Bible, so that Christ's followers can live in accord with God's ways, His Word, and His will (a result of spiritual *maturity*).

These "purposes" echo the internal structures of the Great Commandment (Matthew 22:37-40) and the Great Commission (Matthew 28:19-20).[9] They are already present in most, if not all, churches. But they are not present in a balanced way. Some churches might stress membership over maturity—bad idea. Other churches might have a wonderful maturity program, but at the expense of missions—also not good. A few churches might even forget about ministry altogether and end up with a thousand moms and dads who have no place to put their toddlers during Sunday-morning services—*really* bad. Balance, in other words, is what Warren is advocating.

Balancing God's purposes will result in a healthy church, which in turn will likely cause church growth (not because of any quality of man-centeredness, but because the purposes follow God's biblical pattern). As for numerical attendance, it is secondary, if not tertiary. In fact, it is only one of five ways Warren measures church growth and success:

A church needs to grow *warmer* through fellowship, *deeper* through discipleship, *stronger* through worship, *broader* through ministry, and *larger* through evangelism.[10]

Warren's diamond bases are really nothing more than a "life development process" based on Matthew 22:37-40 and Matthew 28:19-20.[11] These passages actually inspired Warren to come up with one of Saddleback's first mottos: "A Great Commitment to the Great Commandment and the Great Commission will grow a

Great Church."[12] *That* is the purpose-driven church. As Warren has often said, "If you only get two verses in life, get the great commandment and the great commission and you've got the five purposes of God."[13]

## Got Life?

Those two passages from Matthew also undergird *The Purpose-Driven Life,* Warren's next major book, which was written for a three-tiered audience: 1) the unchurched masses; 2) former church members who, for whatever reason, have rejected Christianity (or fallen away); and 3) committed Christians wanting deeper intimacy with God. "It's really about God," Warren asserts—its whole thesis "is that we were made by God and for God. And until we understand that, life isn't going to make any sense."[14] The book's aim is to help people build a spiritually healthy life by either reconnecting with God or connecting with their Creator for the very first time.

And the book's five purposes are based entirely on the Bible:[15]

1. "You were planned for God's pleasure" (Revelation 4:11)

2. "You were formed for God's family" (Romans 8:15; Galatians 4:4-7)

3. "You were created to become like Christ" (Ephesians 5:2; Philippians 2:5; Colossians 3:13; 1 Peter 2:21; 1 John 2:6)

4. "You were shaped for serving God" (Romans 12:1-2)

5. "You were made for a mission" (Matthew 28:19)

Focusing on "purpose" does not detract from the Gospel, since "purpose" can only come from one source: God. And "purpose" can only be accessed through one unique person—Christ, who lived, died, and rose again from the dead for our sins, so that by grace through faith in Him, we could receive new life in the world to come—*and* in this world. The unpleasant alternative was articulated by atheist Bertrand Russell (1872–1970): "Unless you assume God, the question of life's purpose is meaningless."[16]

## Benefits Based on the Bible

How does the emphasis on "purpose" relate to spreading the Good News? Scripture provides many examples of God's people telling about Christ in different ways—using various lead-ins, so to speak: healing (Acts 3:1-6), exposition of Old Testament prophecies (Acts 8:29-38), and appeals to history (Acts 7:2-59). The best preacher, of course, was Jesus. And He "always started with a need, a hurt, or an interest," says Warren. "He never said, 'This is day 54. Let's turn to our Lessons in Deuteronomy 8. We had Deuteronomy 7 last week.' He always started with a practical need."[17]

This is a good point. Jesus healed the sick—a felt need. He changed water into wine—another felt need. He fed the hungry—also a felt need. And He raised the dead—the ultimate felt need. He met people where they were, not where He wanted them to be (as Warren would say it).

Consider Christ's interaction with the Samaritan woman (John 4:7-29). He first opened her eyes to her situation and needs, *then* revealed Himself to her as the answer to her dilemma. And when faced with hungry crowds, Christ did not say, "Let their belly remain empty, for the food I give about my death, burial, and resurrection is all they need, beyond which lieth only heresy, selfishness, and sin-oriented worldly stroking of their felt needs." Instead, He essentially said, "If they're hungry, let's see what you've got. If it's only some fishes and a few loaves of bread, hand them over to Me in faith, and I'll take care of it. Let's get these folks fed."

Consider, too, how "joy" (a feeling) is stressed throughout the New Testament as one of the benefits of living for God. The *Dictionary of Biblical Imagery* explains that Paul and the other New Testament writers communicated to their readers the basic promise that "Christians can live joyfully in a fallen world, during the most intense persecution and through the worst affliction."[18] This is not "the Gospel" in the strictest sense of the term. It is a *result of accepting* the Gospel.

| The Bible | The Purpose-Driven Life |
|---|---|
| • "The wisdom of this world is foolishness with God" (1 Corinthians 3:19). | • "You must turn to God's Word, not the world's wisdom" (page 20). |
| • "What is your life? It is even a vapour" (James 4:14). | • "Life is extremely brief.... Earth is only a temporary residence" (page 47). |
| • "[We seek] a better country, that is, an heavenly [one]" (Hebrews 11:13-16). | • "Your identity is in eternity, and your homeland is heaven" (page 48). |
| • "The invisible things of him from the creation of the world are clearly seen, being understood by the things that are made, even his eternal power and Godhead" (Romans 1:20; see also Psalm 19:1-2). | • "Where is the glory of God?...*Everything* created by God reflects His glory.... We see it everywhere, from the smallest microscopic form of life to the vast Milky Way" (page 53). |

Paul noted, "We glory in tribulations also; knowing that tribulation worketh patience: And patience experience; and experience, hope" (Romans 5:3). And James wrote, "Count it all joy when ye fall into divers [various] temptations [or trials]; knowing this, that the trying of your faith worketh patience. But let patience have her perfect work, that ye may be perfect and entire, wanting nothing" (James 1:2-4).

Likewise, Warren says, "You will be tested by major changes, delayed promises, impossible problems, unanswered prayers, undeserved criticism, and even senseless tragedies....Life is a test....Nothing is insignificant....Every second is a growth opportunity to deepen your character, to demonstrate love, or to depend on God."[19]

This is but one example of the many different truths that *coincide* with the Gospel without *being* the Gospel in the strictest sense (see charts, pages 63 and 65). Warren has rightly picked up on the fact that these truths can often open up people's hearts to the central message of the Good News—the life, death, and resurrection of Jesus.

Obviously, there is a basic correspondence between the Bible and Warren's purpose-driven message. And this is without even taking into consideration the *hundreds* of other statements in *The Purpose-Driven Life* that mirror a plethora of biblical concepts relating to, for instance, God's triune nature, obedience to Christ's commands, the necessity of church involvement, spiritual maturity in Christ, service to God, the importance of prayer—and last, but certainly not least, the Christian's call to evangelism.

It is through us that God accomplishes what He pleases. He, of course, does not *need* to work out His will in such a way. But He *chooses* to do so. It is a sublimely miraculous arrangement wherein He carries out His plans (or His purposes) by first creating us, and then by revealing to us the purposes for which we were created. We carry out *His* purposes by carrying out *our* purposes. It is an ultimate "killing two birds with one stone" course of action—with a divine twist.

Being endowed with a divine purpose is nothing less than a precious gift from our loving Creator who wants us be all that we were meant to be *for His glory* (Isaiah 43:7). God reveals His purposes or plans *to* the world by using us *in* the world. We are, spiritually speaking, the "body" of Christ on earth (1 Corinthians 12:27)—hands, feet, eyes, ears—designed to know Him, obey Him, serve Him, and love Him.

| **The Bible** | *The Purpose-Driven Life* |
|---|---|
| • "Thou shalt love the Lord thy God with all thy heart, and with all thy soul, and with all thy mind" (Matthew 22:37). | • "God doesn't want a part of your life. He asks for *all* your heart, *all* your soul, *all* your mind, and *all* your strength" (page 100). |
| • "Be...merciful, as your Father also is merciful." "Be kind...forgiving one another, even as God for Christ's sake hath forgiven you" (Luke 6:36; Ephesians 4:32). | • "God's mercy to us is the motivation for showing mercy to others. Remember, you will never be asked to forgive someone else more than God has already forgiven you" (page 143). |
| • "Whom he did foreknow, he also did predestinate to be conformed to the image of his Son" (Romans 8:29). | • "From the very beginning, God's plan has been to make you like his Son, Jesus" (page 171). |

In summary, then, Rick Warren is simply asserting that living in, by, for, through, and because of God changes everything. Once someone is saved, adopting God's outlook on life enables them to see the significance of life. They can finally see how they fit into the universal tapestry being woven by God, who alone knows how it will all look. And on top of all that, Christians get to go to heaven—Good News, indeed!

## A Legacy of Love

Many years have passed since Rick and Kay first moved to California. In 2002, Warren was named "America's most influential pastor" by *Christianity Today*. He is now known as a modern Martin Luther, whose ideas have spawned a new reformation.[20]

But in addition to those wonderful markers in Saddleback's history, Rick and Kay have experienced many days of sorrow.

Rick and Kay at home in 2005. "There wouldn't be a Saddleback Church without my wife."

Rick's mother, for instance, passed away unexpectedly in 1996. Not long afterward, his father, Jimmy, was diagnosed with cancer, a disease he fought bravely for many months...until late 1999, when he closed his eyes for the last time and went home to be with Jesus, his longtime Lord.

Jimmy spent his last weeks in Rick's home, fading in and out of cancer-induced deliriums, often dreaming about the past and muttering loudly. The visions always had to do with his endless passion—building churches. His mind took him back to the good old days: to Israel, Russia, Guatemala, Asia, Australia. "You guys take that lumber," he would say from his deathbed. "Make sure the team gets back from lunch on time." "Put that joist over there." "Don't you get electrocuted when you put that socket in."[21]

After Jimmy's death, Rick shared with his congregation how his father had given him a final message during his final days. In the midst of his confusion, not long before he departed for heaven, there was a moment of clarity:

> He kept trying to get out of bed, very agitated, and Kay tried again to calm Jimmy down. "Please lie back down in the bed." Finally, she said, "Jimmy, what are you trying to do? What do you want?" He said, "I've got to reach one more for Jesus. Got to reach one more for Jesus. Got to reach one more for Jesus." He began to say this over and over, and in the next hour, must have repeated it maybe a hundred times. "Got to save one more for Jesus. Reach one more for Jesus." As I sat there by his bedside, I put my head down and began to cry. I was praying and thanking God for the faith of my father. Then my dad reached up and put his hand on my head like a blessing, and he said: "Reach one more for Jesus. Reach one more for Jesus." I intend for that to be the theme of the rest of my life.

Under the sun in Angel Stadium during Saddleback's Twenty-Fifth Anniversary Celebration service (April 17, 2005). Rick and Kay (top and far right) with Don Dale (left, Saddleback's first member and still a member) and his wife (center).

About two years later, Rick Warren published *The Purpose-Driven Life,* and to this day he continues to fulfill his father's dying wish for him to reach the lost with the Gospel of Jesus Christ. Jimmy's legacy continues to be a powerful motivating force behind not only his son Rick, but also Saddleback Church.

There are countless souls who have been changed by God through their exposure to *The Purpose-Driven Life*. At Saddleback I have personally met hundreds of people whose lives bear the mark of godly transformation through the saving love, grace, and mercy of God at work in their hearts via the power of the Holy Spirit.

Despite the tremendous fruit of Warren's ministry, he has not yet enjoyed a year free of harsh criticisms. Such attacks have recently become even more intense, going far beyond the initial allegations in the 1980s that he was a "liberal." He is now being condemned by some critics as one of the worst deceivers to ever hit the church. The many different issues surrounding this backlash against him will be the subject of the next three chapters.

# CHAPTER 4

# A Watered-Down Christianity?

*It's a myth that you must compromise the message*
*to draw a crowd. Jesus certainly didn't. You don't have*
*to transform the message, but you do have to translate it.*

RICK WARREN, *MINISTRY TOOLBOX* (2002),
"LEARNING TO PREACH LIKE JESUS"

The Gospel can be presented in many ways. For example, I might tell a Buddhist about the prophecies fulfilled in Christ's life in order to show how Jesus is the true Messiah. With an atheist, on the other hand, I would likely discuss God by using an "Intelligent Design" argument. Then again, if I were to run across a person who had a cruel earthly father, I might talk to them about our heavenly Father who loves us. Or with a lonely non-Christian, I might refer to Jesus as our Friend who will never forsake us. With the hurting, I could talk to them about the Spirit who comforts us. And even more relevant, if I were to meet someone who felt they had no purpose in life, I would tell them how they could find purpose and meaning in God through Christ.

Moreover, it would be perfectly acceptable to tell someone

exactly what they could expect to receive from God. The *primary* gift is eternal life. But most people, while on this side of heaven, also receive greater peace, previously unknown joy, a reason to live, and answers to some of their problems (financial, marital, and familial, to name but a few). Highlighting these "benefits" of the Gospel to those who are unfamiliar with them is not changing the Gospel. It is explaining the Gospel in a different way.

At this point an analogy may be helpful. Consider a piece of music. At first it may appear rather simple. And indeed, most people hearing a song will just hear a basic melody, or perhaps some harmony. A few might even be able to distinguish between the "verses," the "chorus," and the "bridge." But there is more to music than these things.

Any song—even something as simple as "Happy Birthday"—can be played in such a way as to make it sound like a jazz piece, a concerto by Mozart, a classic rock hit, a medieval chant, or a Broadway show tune. The song itself remains the same. It is still heard as "Happy Birthday." But its quality (and dare I say, its appeal) can be altered by tempo changes, thickening the chord structures with notes complementary to the melody, varying the available harmonies, changing rhythms, and switching the instruments used.

All of these things, metaphorically speaking, can be done to the Gospel. The key, of course, is that someone must still be presenting the true Gospel. But beyond that restriction there is great freedom, except for obvious guidelines such as "speaking the truth in love" with "gentleness and respect" (Ephesians 4:15; 2 Timothy 2:24-26).

All this must be kept in mind in regard to the concerns raised about Rick Warren's presentation of the Gospel. Many of these concerns arise from reasonable mistakes. Others are serious misunderstandings, particularly those that fail to rightly identify the most basic substructure of Warren's faith, which is conservative, evangelical, and Southern Baptist.

## GIVING OUT THE GOOD NEWS

*Not enough mention of hell?* Absent from *The Purpose-Driven Life* "is a clear explanation of the eternal consequences of sin, or why Jesus died on the cross.... Warren does briefly mention hell (on pages 37 and 112), but he does so almost in passing, without emphasizing the gravity of eternal condemnation."[1]

*The response.* On page 37, Warren writes, "Eternity offers only two [choices]: heaven or hell....If you learn to love and trust God's Son, Jesus, you will be invited to spend the rest of eternity with him....If you reject his love, forgiveness, and salvation, you will spend eternity apart from God forever." On page 112, he says: "[You should praise God] for the rest of your life because of what Jesus did for you on the cross. *God's Son died for you!...* Why? So you could be spared from eternity in hell."

Every book (and preacher) that deals with hell does so to a varying degree. So how much "emphasizing the gravity of eternal condemnation" is enough? A page's worth? A chapter's worth? The truth is that thousands of books on hell's intricacies have already been printed and distributed. Consequently, when a Christian uses the term "hell," whoever is reading that particular word likely knows quite well what is being discussed (see also the concern about God's "hate" on pages 117-118).

When, at the age of 17, I was told that if I did not accept Jesus as my Savior I would go to hell, I knew precisely what that meant. No one had to emphasize the seriousness of it to me. Many of today's unbelievers probably don't need it emphasized either. What they need to know is how to *escape* it. So Warren quickly moves on to the Good News—the possibility of an eternity with God and new life in Christ!

*Parts of the Gospel missing?* The Gospel "deals with God's law, His grace, human depravity, redemption from sin, justification, sanctification, holiness, the nature of saving faith, and the lordship of Christ. And the true gospel's most essential features are the cross of Christ and the truth of the resurrection. None of those subjects is dealt with adequately or biblically in *The Purpose-Driven Life*."[2]

*The response.* Warren's book is a devotional meant to help people focus on God, not analyze Gospel truths. Still, he does mention in brief most of the issues listed above, despite the fact that they go significantly deeper than the *basic* Gospel (which is Christ's life, death, and resurrection).[3]

But why did Warren write his book? What message is he offering? Where is he seeking to meet people? These are questions that cannot be dismissed. No book discusses every issue perfectly or to its greatest depths. There will always be more to say. Hence, there is no end to books (Ecclesiastes 12:12).

The main concerns of readers of *The Purpose-Driven Life* are going to be very basic: "What do I do now? Where can I find hope? How can I get through another day?" These are the questions Warren seeks to answer. He is simply explaining that salvation involves people receiving or accepting Christ by faith as their Savior (see John 1:12). As Joshua told the people of Israel, "Choose ye this day whom ye will serve" (Joshua 24:15).

How is *The Purpose-Driven Life* affecting people in general? Is it drawing them to the only true God of the Bible, who revealed Himself in the person and work of Jesus Christ, by whose death on the cross we are redeemed from sin and death? For many readers, the answer to this question would be a resounding *yes*.

---

*Making God too "safe"?* "Warren's explanation of God leaves out many important truths and emphasizes those qualities that make God feel close and safe....You will never hear about God's wrath....You will never hear the warnings in the Bible about God's coming judgment. You will not learn about God's holiness....[His] portrayal of God's nature is not complete....[He] does not fully represent who God is."[4]

---

*The response.* If Warren emphasizes those attributes that make God "feel close and safe," perhaps it is because the church has for too many decades been overemphasizing those attributes that make Him feel distant and unsafe. Unbelievers know precious little about God's love, grace, and mercy. Nor do they have any clear concept of what it is like to be a Christian: having the joyful expectation of one day seeing Christ, the peaceful assurance that our heavenly Father is in control, and the comforting support of the Spirit through suffering. *Balance* about God is what Warren is seeking to create.

Even so, his book does deal with God's wrath, as well as sin and holiness. Chapter 26 is devoted entirely to sanctification—

"Growing Through Temptation." It reveals that Satan tempts us to sin, that sinful desire *within us* is the root of temptation, and that doubting God (or succumbing to temptation) leads to sin.[5] Warren even includes a lengthy section on "Overcoming Temptation," and then follows that up with yet another chapter on holiness, titled "Defeating Temptation."

*God needs us?* In Warren's chapter "Becoming Best Friends with God," God is made to look "as if He were in need, 'Almighty God yearns to be your Friend!'...meaning He needs to be your Friend."[6]

*The response.* Warren's book actually says that "God didn't *need* to create you. He wasn't lonely" and "you were formed for God's family....[But] God didn't *need* a family."[7] His remark about God yearning for us no more misrepresents God's nature than any of the similar comments that have been made over the years by countless Christians from varying denominations (see endnote 8).[8] Words like "yearns," "desires," and "wants" simply express in human terms the Lord's wish that none should perish (2 Peter 3:9).

## DOCTRINE THAT COUNTS

Christians are united (or should be united) by a set of shared beliefs in the doctrines that really count. These are usually referred to as the "essentials" of the faith, which are any beliefs that relate directly to one's identification of, and relationship to, God. Among such beliefs are the biblical teachings about God, the Trinity, the virgin birth of Christ, the full humanity and deity of Jesus, the atonement, salvation by grace alone through faith alone, and the bodily resurrection of Jesus after His crucifixion.

Nonessentials of the faith include everything else. In this grouping we find a great diversity of thought about baptism, gifts of the Spirit, the "end times," how a church should be governed, Bible versions, "proper" clothing, use of instruments in worship services, and a host of other topics. Some of the greatest theologians, Bible teachers, and Christian workers in history have disagreed on these and other issues.

Sadly, some Christians place far too much emphasis on nonessentials, using them to criticize fellow believers, sometimes accusing them of not even being Christian. But our intentions should be guided by doctrinal balance, fair-mindedness, discernment, and love. In looking at Rick Warren, then, what does he actually teach? What does he not teach? What is the *whole message* he is communicating, as opposed to what isolated words or sentences can be made to seem to say?

**Doctrine is unimportant?** "According to Warren, 'God won't ask about your religious background or doctrinal views...(*PDL*, p. 34)....But apart from Bible doctrine about the Person and work of Christ, we might put our faith in the wrong 'Christ.'"[9]

*The response.* Warren is not dismissing the importance of a biblically sound understanding of Jesus' true identity. He is only seeking to dispel the *false* notions that 1) God is going to accept a person's religious upbringing as an excuse for not accepting Christ; 2) denominational affiliation and pet doctrines are effective substitutes for a relationship to Jesus as one's personal Lord and Savior; and 3) in order to accept Jesus as Lord and Savior, a person must first have all of their doctrinal "ducks in a row."

Right after the comment quoted above, Warren offers Christ's declaration: "*I am the way and the truth and the life. No one comes to the Father except through me* [John 14:6]." A few paragraphs later he expands on the remark: "While life on earth offers many choices, eternity only offers two: heaven or hell. Your relationship to God on earth will determine your relationship to him in eternity." He then points out that only by loving and trusting Jesus will anyone be "invited to spend the rest of eternity with him." The alternative, he says, is "eternity apart from God forever."[10] That is the basic Gospel.

## Saving Faith

It is here that a word must be said about how Warren preaches to the unsaved. He firmly believes that people do not need to have everything figured out before they can receive Christ as their Lord and Savior. Saving faith, in fact, can be as simple as the faith expressed by a child (Mark 10:15; Luke 18:15-17). According to Warren, doctrinal depth will come in time as new believers are guided into spiritual maturity by God's voice and through the study of Scripture. But first they have to become Christians.[11]

Even the prominent Walter Martin (1928–1989)—acknowledged father of the modern countercult movement—made such allowances. In his book *Essential Christianity*, he quoted the Princeton theologian J. Gresham Machen (1881–1937), staunch defender of orthodoxy:

> Who can tell exactly how much knowledge of the facts about Christ is necessary if a man is to have saving faith? None but God can tell. Some knowledge is cer-

tainly required, but how much is required we cannot say.[12]

Anthony Hoekema (1913–1988)—the well-respected Reformed theologian—also gave a rather Warren-esque opinion in *The Four Major Cults* (see note 13).[13]

*The Purpose-Driven Life* is a basic evangelistic tool, and as such, presents a basic Gospel message that does not explore or refute the inexhaustible number of false Christs preached by other religious belief systems. Warren's concern and calling—as a pastor—is simply preaching Jesus to the crowds using a "Come to Christ" appeal. He constantly stresses the need for *relationship* with Jesus as opposed to following a *religion*—be it Hinduism, Buddhism, Mormonism, Judaism, or any other "ism," including Protestantism and Roman Catholicism.[14]

*Keeping Purpose in Perspective*

The *Purpose-Driven Life* is not a book of systematic theology, nor was it ever intended to be one. Warren's volume is a devotional guide. It is meant first for unbelievers, then for those who have fallen away from a vibrant relationship with God—and finally, for the average, non-seminary-trained Christian seeking a simple daily reading plan.

Consequently, Warren puts his emphasis on just two main things: 1) helping Christians refocus their sights on Jesus, the author and finisher of their faith (Hebrews 12:2); and 2) getting unbelievers to think about God, Jesus, and their need to have a relationship with Christ.

Though Warren's devotional is not targeting in-depth theological instruction, this does not mean his view of doctrine is low. It is quite high, not only because he believes it is important, but also because he knows it is necessary. But he is careful to not engage in doctrinal overkill.

Jesus, it must be remembered, did not say, "And this is life eternal, that they might know *about* thee, the only true God, and Jesus Christ." He said, "That they may *know* thee" (John 17:3). Warren's book is an introduction to God so people can get to know Him—not know merely *about* Him. As A.W. Tozer said, "A doctrine has practical value only as far as it is prominent in our thoughts and makes a difference in our lives."[15]

*Digging Deeper*

As for doctrine at Saddleback, one need only go to the church's Web site at saddleback.com and Warren's Web site www.pastors.com. Both reveal a deep commitment to doctrine and its relationship to spiritual maturity. For example, since 1993 Warren's longtime assistant pastor (and brother-in-law), Tom Holladay, has been teaching on a regular basis (along with Kay Warren) a doctrinal series currently titled "Foundations: 11 Core Truths to Build Your Life On." It covers eleven Christian doctrines: the Bible, God, Jesus, the Holy Spirit, creation, salvation, sanctification, good and evil, the afterlife, the church, and the second coming.

In the pastors.com article "Why Doctrine Matters to Your Members," Holladay and Kay Warren plainly note the view of Saddleback: "Doctrine is what God says about the most important aspects of our lives." They go on to list various reasons why doctrine is important, including, "Because knowing the truth about God helps me know God better," "Because doctrine feeds my soul," "Because knowing the truth protects against error," "Because I am commanded to study the truth," "Because I am commanded to live the truth," "Because I am commanded to defend the truth."[16]

Another pastors.com article, "Biblical Doctrine Is Practical and Life-Changing," notes that "biblical doctrine—or a biblical worldview—is one of the most practical, life-changing things that pastors can teach their congregations. Doctrine is simply what the Bible says about God, and it is something that should impact how we live our lives."[17]

> *Purpose-driven—an esoteric philosophy?* It "is a surrogate theological paradigm, replacing the old traditional doctrines about the nature of man and God....[It] is derived from esoteric philosophies prevalent in the 1800s... most notably Theosophy."[18]

*The response.* The *Purpose-Driven Life* refers to God's five "purposes" for us (see page 61). Warren's book also uses traditional Christian terms—and the traditional meanings behind those terms—for man's sinful nature and the triune God (including several divine attributes). For example, he notes the miraculous and undeserved relationship we can have with God: "It's difficult to imagine how an intimate friendship is possible between an omnipotent, invisible, perfect God and a finite, sinful human being."[19]

*Overcoming the Great Divide*

With regard to the depravity of man, Warren believes that every non-Christian is a sinner separated by his or her sin from a personal God. He has explained this bedrock Christian concept using classic terminology for original sin:

> Everybody has sinned, and we're all to be condemned because of that....Adam was a real person and because of his disobedience sin entered the world....There are two diabolical twins—sin and death. One goes with the

> other. When you see one you'll see the other. Death is
> a direct result of sin. The Bible says, "The wages of sin
> is death." What is death? There are actually three dif-
> ferent kinds of death as the Bible teaches: 1) physical
> death...2) spiritual death...3) eternal death.[20]

Warren has never avoided teaching that *everyone's* fundamental
and inescapable problem is the "sin nature." Saddleback's Web site
explains, "Every person, although endowed with the image of God,
inherited a disobedient heart from Adam, the very first man. This
attitude of disobedience (called sin in the Bible)—unless rectified
through Christ—forever keeps man from forming a relationship
with his Creator." The consequences of our sin nature can *only* be
removed by accepting Christ as personal Lord and Savior (see the
interview for more about this). Why? Because "Jesus died and rose
to pay for our sins." Warren explains, "It's His death and resurrection, that's the most important part."[21]

## One What and Three Whos

As for Warren's theology, he is an orthodox Trinitarian who
upholds the traditional Christian belief that God's nature "is rela-
tional" in terms of three distinct Persons: Father, Son, and Holy
Spirit. "The Trinity is God's relationship to Himself "—"God
invites us to enjoy friendship and fellowship with all three persons of the Trinity: our Father, the Son, and the Holy Spirit."[22]

Saddleback's Web site uses a traditional definition of God's
nature: "Although it might be difficult for the human mind to
comprehend, the Bible teaches that He is one yet has existed
since the beginning of time as three distinct and equal persons:
the Father, the Son and the Holy Spirit."[23] The church's dedication
to historic trinitarianism is indisputable and nonnegotiable, as the
"Foundations" course makes clear:

God exists as a Trinity....God is three in one—Father, Son, and Holy Ghost. He is not three Gods [polytheism], nor is he one God acting in three different ways [modalism]....God is three different and distinct persons...[who] are one in the being of God.[24]

As for Theosophy (founded by occultist Helena Blavatsky, 1831–1891), it is about as far away from Warren's faith as is possible. Blavatsky's religion is a metaphysical mix of spiritualism, pseudoscience, Transcendentalism, and belief in the powers of positive thought (or mental healing). It helped spread Eastern philosophy in America and, along with various other groups, gave rise to the "New Age Movement."

***Warren the Arminian?*** He "holds to an Arminian view of the Gospel." "The Arminian view of God electing mankind is demonstrated perfectly in the PDL."[25]

***The response.*** Troubling this critic is Warren's failure to advance the doctrine of "limited atonement," which teaches that Christ's death provided atonement *only* for the elect—those who are predestined by God to be saved. (This is one of the "five points" of Calvinism, which is an alternative to Arminianism.)[26]

But Warren's views, according to Saddleback associate pastor Tom Holladay, are "classic Southern Baptist."[27] This is significant since the official statement of faith produced by the Southern Baptist Convention ("Baptist Faith and Message," 2000), upholds several aspects of Calvinism, including man's depravity (sinful nature), the unconditional election (choosing) of certain persons for salvation, and the perseverance (eternal security) of the saints.

Warren cannot be classed as an Arminian, most obviously

because Arminianism teaches that Christians can lose their salvation. But Warren and Saddleback *strongly* reject this teaching. The saddleback.com Web page reads: "If I accept Jesus Christ, is my salvation forever? Definitely! Your salvation is through the most trustworthy being in the universe—Jesus Christ! You didn't do anything to earn your salvation, and you can't do anything to lose it."[28]

## NOT SO SOFT ON SIN

*No repentance?* Missing from Warren's books and from the messages being preached in "our Churches today is the message of contrition and true repentance."[29]

*The response.* According to Warren,

- "The ultimate paradigm shift is repentance."
- "Repentance is change at the deepest level."
- "[You] don't change people's minds. The applied Word of God does."
- "The deepest kind of preaching is preaching for repentance."
- "Repentance is the central theme of the New Testament."[30]

He has explained at his Purpose-Driven conferences how to teach repentance uncompromisingly:

Do I ever preach repentance? Of course I preach repentance. That's the basic message of the New Testament—repentance....You ask, "How do you preach on a negative passage?" With a humble, loving attitude—not superior to your hearers. We're all in the same boat. When you preach on a negative passage you confess, "I've fallen short here, too." Change the pronouns from "you" to "we."[31]

In other words, Warren tweaks his presentation of repentance not by softening it, but by counting himself among the world-wide mass of sinners for whom Christ died. He has always taught that preaching on repentance and hell *must* be presented with a broken spirit, a grieving heart, and a humble attitude—"not with a smile on your face." He adds, "All of us have sinned, everybody has blown it. Everybody comes short of God's glory. It's a fact of life, folks. I don't measure up to my own standards, much less God's."

*No sin?* "Purpose-Driven Life doctrine deal[s] with sin not at all."[32]

*The response. The Purpose-Driven Life* tells us, "Receive Jesus into your life as your Lord and Savior. Receive his forgiveness for your sins." "God proves his love for us in that while we still were sinners Christ died for us." "Jesus took all of mankind's sin and guilt on himself." "The church is made up of real sinners, including ourselves....Every church could put out a sign 'No perfect people need apply. This is a place only for those who admit they are sinners, need grace, and want to grow.'"[33]

*No preaching against sin?* "Warren freely admits that he never preaches against homosexuality, abortion, or any type of sin for that matter....He believes it's wrong, but he would never say it from behind the pulpit."[34]

***The response.*** Warren has admitted no such thing. Consider what he said, for example, in a pulpit sermon titled "Maintaining Moral Purity":

> God's standard has never changed. Premarital sex is unacceptable to God. It always has been. It always will be. Living together without getting married is unacceptable to God. It always has been. It always will be. Adultery, having an affair, being unfaithful to somebody you're married to is unacceptable to God. It always has been and it always will be. Homosexuality is unacceptable to God. It always has been. It always will be. Pornography is unacceptable to God. It always has been. It always will be.
>
> Every one of those things brings a judgment. If you have been guilty of one or all of these things I've just mentioned you've come to the right place. This is what Saddleback's all about. A place for healing, forgiveness, restoration. God says, *I want to give you a chance to come clean and start over and make the rest of your life the best of your life*....What is the pathway back to purity? 1) Repent. Repent means "to change your mind."...It means I change my mind and say, "You were right, God. It was wrong. It's sin." I don't rationalize it. I don't excuse it. I don't say everybody's doing it. I say, "It was wrong."[35]

At Saddleback, "seeker-sensitive" does not mean condoning sin. It simply means talking about sin in a way that seekers *and saints* can understand it and its ramifications in life. As Warren says, "A Christian does not stop being a human the moment he's born again. So he still has the same problems that unbelievers do [that is to say, temptations, sin, and the trials of life]. That's what you focus on in a seeker-sensitive service."[36]

This is *not* a "feel-good kind of approach," as Pastor John MacArthur phrased it during his CNN-broadcast criticisms. He further alleged of Warren, "This is telling people exactly what they want to hear, telling people that God agrees with you. God wants you to be what you want to be. And this is pretty heady stuff, to tell somebody that the God of the universe wants them to be exactly what they want to be."[37]

But what Warren actually has said about what God wants for us is something quite different: "You become *what God made you to be*....You will never be fully satisfied in life until you begin to be *what God made you to be*....Find out *what God made you to be* and be it....You cannot conform to the will of man if you're going to be *what God wants you to be*...."[38] This is the standard Saddleback message—life in Christ is equated with letting go of what *you* want to be and embracing whatever *God* wants you to be.

CHAPTER 5

# A New Spirituality?

*One of the most amazing things to me is the popularity of the New Age Movement. It takes more faith to believe in that than it does to believe in Christianity. It is the most illogical, irrational thing.*

RICK WARREN, OCTOBER 8, 1989,
"GOD'S PURPOSE FOR YOUR LIFE"

Warren has consistently maintained that no religious figure, or cult leader, or self-help motivational speaker is ever going to get people into an eternity with God. His desire is, and always has been, to connect people to the biblical Christ, as He is defined by the historic, orthodox creeds of Christendom—God the Son, the Second Person of the Holy Trinity. And *this* Jesus, according to Warren, is the only way of salvation:

> Sometimes people say, "How can you say that Jesus is the only way?" I didn't say it. Jesus did. He said, *"I am the Way, the Truth, and the Life. No one comes unto the Father but by Me."* If you have a problem with that, you don't have a problem with me. You have a problem with Jesus. I would suggest you had better check

it out because He's either a liar or He's telling the truth, and you're betting your eternity on it.[1]

Warren's unwillingness to blur doctrinal lines relating to the essentials of Christianity has been made clear, as has Saddleback Church's commitment to maintaining and defending historic Christianity.

## GUILT BY ASSOCIATION

*Promoting false teachers?* Warren quotes questionable persons: Bernie Siegel, Henry David Thoreau, George Bernard Shaw, Mother Teresa, Madame Guyon, and Albert Schweitzer.[2] He is obviously "promoting false teachers."[3]

*The response.* Warren quotes *many* non-Christians and people of other religious traditions in his books and sermons. Is it because he agrees with them on everything? No. Is it because he is promoting them as examples of sound Christians? No. He is showing that all "truth"—wherever it may be found—is God's truth.

Christians as far back as the first century were quoting pagans in hopes of communicating the truths of the Gospel. They saw that unbelievers, including the Greek philosophers, had made astute observations about God and possessed some truths consistent with Christianity. In the Gospel of John, for instance, we find the Greek word *logos* ("Word") being used to describe Jesus. *Logos* was a Greek philosophical term that represented "reason" as a sort of bridge between the unreachable God and earthly matter. Hence, Jesus, as the eternal *logos,* is the bridge between God and man.

Moreover, the apostle Paul made significant appeals to non-Christian sources as a way of illuminating Christian truths. In his sermon to the Athenians (Acts 17:22-34), he mentions their altar to "THE UNKNOWN GOD," saying, "Whom therefore ye ignorantly worship, him declare I unto you." He concluded, "[God is] not far from every one of us: For in him we live and move, and have our being; as certain also of your own poets have said, For we are also his offspring."

Paul's words "we live and move, and have our being" are from a poem by the pagan Epimenides of Crete (around 600 BC) to the Supreme God. And Paul's assertion, "For we are also his offspring," is from *Phenomena* by the pagan poet Aratus of Cilicia (third century BC), which in turn reflects the teachings of Cleanthes, a Stoic philosopher (also third century BC). Paul then cites Epimenides again in Titus 1:12. And in 1 Corinthians 15:33 he uses a proverb from *Thaïs* (a comedy by the Greek playwright Menander, 342–292 BC).

Warren is doing nothing less—and nothing more—than Paul.

*Other religions are Christian "denominations."* In a July 21, 2004, *USA Today* report by Cathy Lynn Grossman, "we read how Warren operates: 'Warren's pastor-training programs welcome Catholics, Methodists, Mormons, Jews and ordained women.' 'I'm not going to get into a debate over the non-essentials. I won't try to change other denominations.'…Refusal to quibble over what he considers 'non-essentials' has indeed won him friends in camps that are doctrinally aberrant on essentials."[4] "Warren's confusion about the Gospel is shown also in that he extends his

Purpose-Driven seminars to include Catholics and even Mormons.... [H]e must see some good in their systems of doctrine."[5] Warren encourages everyone to attend his pastor-training programs, including Mormons.[6]

***The response.*** According to Brian Davis, manager of Customer Care, Purpose Driven, no Mormons have ever been through any purpose-driven pastor-training conferences or classes—according to all records. More importantly, Warren has never said that his programs "welcome" Mormons. His comment relates only to "denominations." The reference to "Mormons" (and "Jews") was actually the *interpretation* made by *USA Today* of what Warren meant by "denominations."

I learned this through several e-mails exchanged with Cathy Lynn Grossman on April 8, 2005, and a telephone conversation with her on April 27. The *USA Today* writer told me that she, quite innocently, penned her story for a *secular* media outlet using Webster's definition of "denomination"—that is to say, a "religious group." It was *she* who chose the "denominations" (or religious groups) to list, believing they sounded best in the article. Warren himself, however, did not say—and indeed, he is not quoted as saying—that he views Mormons, Jews, or both as simply other "denominations."

*Saddleback vs. Pluralism*

Warren views neither Mormonism, nor Judaism, as just other denominations. Judaism—like Buddhism, Hinduism, and Islam— is another world religion. And as for Mormons, consider what Warren has said in his sermons about that group (and other non-traditional and nonmainstream religious faiths):[7]

- "Paul says they were zealous but 'their zeal is not based on knowledge.' That describes a lot of cults and religions today. A lot of Jehovah's Witness are zealous without knowledge, and Mormons, [and] Moonies. Paul says they are zealous but they don't really know the truth."

- "I'm not going to let any Mormon outwitness me! I *do* believe we should be doing for the truth what people will do for lies." (This is a classic countercult saying popularized by Walter Martin—see page 76.)

As for cults and apologetics, Saddleback offers ongoing classes, conferences, and studies for members. I organized and spoke at Saddleback's "Cult Conference" in the late 1990s, which featured such respected apologists as Alan Gomes (Talbot School of Theology), Bob and Gretchen Passantino (Answers in Action Ministry), and H. Wayne House (Professor of Biblical and Theological Studies, Faith Seminary). And I have lectured on cults and false religious systems at various Purpose-Driven conferences.[8]

*Forget about doctrinal purity?* In *The Purpose-Driven Life*, Warren "*never* warns the believer to watch out for false doctrine or harmful fellowships. He minimizes the need for doctrinal purity by stressing the importance of 'love' and 'unity.' "[9]

*The response.* Warren, in the strongest possible terms, has said the exact opposite on many occasions (also see the previous concern). One of the things he warned his congregation about in a 1997 sermon was syncretism and pluralism—that is to say, the merging for the sake of unity any and all religious beliefs:

I need to warn you of what's called syncretism.... [It's]

the idea of combining a bunch of ideas from many different philosophies and ways of life, put them all together and that will become your philosophy. That becomes your religion. What happens when you take a little bit of Christianity, a little bit of what the Bible says, you take a little bit of Eastern thought, Buddhism, Taoism, throw in a little science fiction, throw in a little more of high technology and what do you get when you mix all that together? You get Heaven's Gate [a cult]....People do this all the time today. They think this is just as legitimate as any other way. The so-called New Age has nothing new about it at all. There is not one single new idea in this New Age thinking. All it is is a combination of very old lies that have been around for centuries, named by other things—paganism, naturalism, pantheism and all these different things. You reformulate them, throw them all in and go out on a limb and you've got New Age. God says, *Don't do that. It's just a combination of old lies.*[10]

Despite such condemnations, Warren continues to be labeled as a false teacher who is seeking to advance the New Age movement, which is basically a blend of ancient occultism, Eastern philosophy, and watered-down pseudo-Christian ideas. The New Age movement, as one writer has explained, is "an extremely large, loosely structured network of organizations and individuals bound together by common values (based in mysticism and monism—the world view that 'all is one') and a common vision (a coming 'new age' of peace and mass enlightenment, the 'Age of Aquarius')."[11] Such beliefs are clearly not held by Warren. Nevertheless, they continue to be attributed to him. Perhaps the most common accusation being voiced is that Warren advocates a kind of "all roads lead to God" philosophy. But nothing could be further from the truth.

## ALL ROADS DO NOT LEAD TO GOD

*A New Age PEACE?* New Agers have declared a "5-Step 'PEACE Plan' to ultimately save the world through the establishment of a 'New Spirituality.'" This PEACE Plan "will help everyone move past 'outmoded' beliefs and prepare the way for the New Spirituality." Warren has initiated his own 5-step P.E.A.C.E. Plan. "Why would God 'do peace' by inspiring a Christian leader to use a similar 5-Step P.E.A.C.E. Plan format as that of a New Age leader?" "Would God inspire a 'Christian' leader to use the same five-step plan format as that of a New Age leader whose five-step peace plan is totally antagonistic to the Bible's true Gospel?...No, He would not!"[12]

*The response.* Warren's P.E.A.C.E. Plan has nothing to do with any kind of New Age manifesto that happens to go by the same name (see pages 22–24 in the interview). Warren's goal is not to advance some New Spirituality. He is seeking to invade the world with Christian spirituality using a fivefold plan: **P**lant churches, **E**quip servant leaders, **A**ssist the poor, **C**are for the sick, and **E**ducate the next generation. This plan was initiated on April 17, 2005, at Saddleback's Twenty-Fifth Anniversary Celebration service in Angel Stadium. The jointly agreed-to declaration was read to all 30,000 people in attendance:

I will live the rest of my life serving God's purposes

with God's people on God's planet for God's glory....I'll do the best I can with what I have for Jesus Christ today....To my Lord and Savior Jesus Christ, I say: However, whenever, wherever, and whatever you ask me to do, my answer in advance is yes!...I want to be used by you in such a way that on that final day I'll hear you say, "Well done, thou good and faithful one."

Warren is not interested in spreading anything but the unde-filed Gospel of Christ. In Saddleback Church's basic C.L.A.S.S. 101 membership course, he makes this very clear:

Buddhism says truth is found through an eightfold path....Hindu scripture says truth is very illusive and you'll probably never find it....Others say truth must be searched for by purifying yourself by chanting.... Mohammed said, "I'm a prophet and I point toward the truth."...[But Jesus] said, "I am the Truth. I am the Way. I am the only way to heaven." God, Himself, came to earth as a human being to bring us back to Himself....The Way is not a religion, the Way is not a path, the Way is a person.[13]

In C.L.A.S.S. 101, Warren also declares that "every single person in the world needs Jesus Christ...needs to have a relationship with Him. If they don't they will spend eternity in hell." This fits well with his P.E.A.C.E. Plan, the purpose of which is to "bring worldwide revival." Warren's new reformation goal is to change "not our beliefs," but "our behavior" toward the world's "hungry, hopeless, and helpless."[14]

> ***Warren is a pantheist?*** "[He writes] 'The Bible says, *He rules everything and is everywhere and is in everything.*'...But is God really 'in everything' as the NCV [New Century Version] and the New Agers teach?...[God] is not 'in everything' and everything is not divine, which is the teaching of pantheism."[15] "Warren is now teaching what all New Agers are teaching—God is in everyone and everything."[16]

***The response.*** Warren's use of Ephesians 4:6 in *The Purpose-Driven Life* is an attempt to teach God's immanence. The thrust of the passage is God's presence not only above and beyond the universe, but also throughout it (His omnipresence). Warren *nowhere* says that everything is "divine" (a word that the writer of the first quote above inserts). Nor does Warren's quoting the New Century Version have anything to do with planting pantheism in the minds of his readers.

In a 1988 sermon, Warren stated that God "can be in many, many places all at the same time. He's everywhere. That does not mean that God is everything. That's pantheism. Don't confuse the creator with His creation. He's not everything but He is everywhere."[17] And consider these remarks from a 1997 sermon:

Another really popular image or idol of God today is "God is the Force." "May the Force be with you."...A lot of people buy into that. It's real popular today. God is an energy force. This energy force flows around us and in us....God flows through everybody and everything.

> Everything is in God, and God is in everything. In fact,
> God's in me, so I'm god! That's exactly what Shirley
> MacLaine and a bunch of other people teach. You're
> god!…You're not God and you know it. You're just
> kidding yourself. God is not in everything. You hear
> this all the time. Everything is in God and God's in
> everything. That's a bunch of baloney! God is not in
> everything. God created everything. No doubt about
> that. But God is not in everything and everything is not
> God. That is called pantheism.[18]

Even in *The Purpose-Driven Life*, Warren denounces today's "many religions and New Age philosophies" that teach what he calls Satan's oldest lie: "that we are divine or can become gods." He also writes, "Let me be absolutely clear: You will never become God, or even *a* god," then adds, "God doesn't want you to become a god; he wants you to become *godly*."[19]

Warren clearly condemns both pantheism and polytheism.[20] Many New Agers, unfortunately, have not only picked up on, but now regularly use, a variety of Christian terms, concepts, phrases, and words: for example, "the Christ," "Word," "transformed," "Lord," and "meditate," to name but a few. It seems that ex–New Ager Christians, perhaps because of their former days in the movement, are oversensitive to any words or phrases that remind them of their years without Christ (see note 21 for one example).[21]

*Mystical practices?* Warren "dabbles in Catholic contemplative prayer techniques, which border on the occult and Eastern meditation," even "quoting Catholic mystic Brother Lawrence and his book *Practicing the Presence of*

*God."* And he endorses Benedictine monks, who, like Brother Lawrence, engaged in "contemplative mysticism."[22]

*The response.* Nowhere in Warren's book does he endorse, refer to, positively mention, or "dabble in" contemplative prayer.[23] Moreover, a computer search I made of almost every sermon Warren has preached since 1984 uncovered no mention of either contemplative prayer or the relatively modern contemplative-prayer movement.

The word "contemplatives" does appear in *The Purpose-Driven Life,* but only once, on page 103: "*Contemplatives* love God through adoration." This is a description of how some people like to worship God and, in context, is set against various other ways that Christians prefer to worship God depending on their personality. For example, care-givers show their love for God by "loving others and meeting needs." Others demonstrate their faith by "confronting evil, battling injustice, and working to make the world a better place" (like countercult ministers or prolife activists). Intellectual believers express worship to God "by studying with their minds." By "contemplatives," Warren simply means people who gravitate toward more emotional and/or internal experiences of communion with God—not necessarily "contemplative prayer."

As for Brother Lawrence (who lived from about 1605 to 1691), he was a Roman Catholic whose *Letters* and *Conversations* (written long before the contemplative-prayer movement) were published as *Practicing the Presence of God.* There is a wealth of wisdom in this volume. Many Protestants, even evangelicals, have recommended it. For example, A.W. Tozer—one of Christianity's most celebrated preachers—wrote that Brother Lawrence "expressed the highest moral wisdom" in discussing sin and forgiveness.[24]

Nevertheless, Brother Lawrence is vilified by assorted fundamentalists simply because 1) he was a Roman Catholic; and 2) he used terminology that would eventually bear a passing resemblance to words and phrases now employed by New Agers. But he lived long before there was any New Age—and before there was any contemplative-prayer movement. His writings are actually quite God-centered.[25]

The point of *Practicing the Presence of God* relates to our need for constant awareness of God. Brother Lawrence stressed that everything should be done, even menial tasks, "for the love of God, and thus achiev[ing] a condition in which the presence of God is as real in work as in prayer."[26] This is why Warren refers to him when telling readers of his book that they should pray "without ceasing." Christians, according to Warren, should "carry on a continuous, open-ended conversation" with God all day, "talking with him about whatever you are doing or thinking," even "while shopping, driving, working, or performing any other everyday tasks."[27]

What about Warren's alleged endorsement of Roman Catholicism and Benedictine monks? All he says in *The Purpose-Driven Life* is that monks "use the hourly chimes of a clock to remind them to pause and pray 'the hour prayer.' If you have a watch or cell phone with an alarm, you could do the same."[28] This is not much of an endorsement of Roman Catholicism in general, or the Benedictines in particular. Besides, the practice of hourly prayer goes back to long before the Benedictine Order was founded (AD 529) and before Roman Catholicism as we know it today even existed! Hours of prayer—initially placed at 9 AM, noon, and 3 PM, then midnight, as well as at the beginning of the day and night—are mentioned *prior to the fourth century* by the church fathers Tertullian, Cyprian, Justin Martyr, and Clement of Alexandria.[29]

## THE SCHULLER STORY

Some of the most impassioned and persistent criticisms against Rick Warren have involved his supposed alliance with Robert Schuller (also see Warren's interview, pages 29–30)—even to the point of CNN's describing Schuller as Warren's mentor (*Larry King Live,* March 14, 2005). In my first interview with Warren (on April 12, 2005), he expressed clear frustration over the incessant linking of him to Schuller, calling it one of the "most overblown" things he has ever come up against. We spent the next 45 minutes talking about Schuller and their "relationship." He then granted me permission to access his personal files that contained private correspondence between him and Schuller.

"Can I quote from these letters?" I asked him.

"Yeah, sure," he answered. "I don't care. Go ahead. You can quote whatever you like. I have nothing to hide."

> ***Mentored by Schuller?*** "Much of the mystery concerning Warren's purpose-driven theology can be cleared up when we realize the source of his ideas"—Robert Schuller, who is Warren's "revered colleague." "Warren is a devotee of Robert Schuller, having attended his pastoral training course many times." "He is Rick Warren's mentor."[30]

*The response.* All of the above concerns are groundless. Unlike Warren, Schuller has in *many* areas stepped well outside the bounds of biblical Christianity and into the realm of heresy and pseudo-Christian teachings. He embraces religious pluralism, for instance, believing that it is wrong to ask those in other religions to abandon their faith in favor of Christianity. Schuller also views as acceptable the use of mantras and Transcendental Meditation (New Age); he advocates "positive thinking" as a path to wholeness and spiritual healing (Mind Science beliefs); he sees "self-love" as spiritually freeing; and he denies traditional Christian definitions of salvation, sin, the sinful state of man, and original sin.

Contrary to the information that has been spread by the secular media and Warren's critics, Warren did not even meet Schuller until many years into Saddleback's history. Of course, prior to meeting him, Warren certainly knew about him—ever since the summer of 1978, when he was still attending Southwestern Theological Seminary (see chapter 1).

According to Warren, he spent the better part of his last two years at the school going around the country to attend seminars being offered by *many* church growth leaders, including Robert Schuller, as was pointed out by *Christianity Today:*

> He and Kay drove west to visit Robert Schuller's Institute for Church Growth. "We had a very stony ride out to the conference," she says, because such nontraditional ministry scared her to death. Schuller, though, won them over. "He had a profound influence on Rick," Kay says. "We were captivated by his positive appeal to nonbelievers."[31]

Far too many inferences have been drawn from this paragraph, even though it only says 1) Schuller's ministry was nontraditional, and 2) Schuller's "positive appeal to unbelievers" was so captivating that it encouraged Warren to also take a nontraditional approach to doing church. In other words, Warren saw that "church" did not have to be done in the same way it had always been done. It was a profound realization.

## The Kay Quote

Kay's "profound influence" remark has been routinely and unreasonably expanded to include Schuller's doctrinal teachings. But an analysis of the sermons in which Warren even mentions Schuller shows that the "influence" exerted on him relates *only* to creative ways in which Schuller built a nontraditional church and to some of Schuller's observations about the unchurched.

For example, in one sermon Warren mentions how Schuller initially had no church building. But he kept looking for one, rather than just giving up, and eventually settled for a drive-in theater! This impressed Warren as a mark of "creativity," a great trait for a church leader to possess. He also has commented on Schuller's apparent ability to look beyond common logistical problems that arise in any church situation.[32]

And one of Warren's 1980 questions to the unchurched— "Why do you think most people don't attend church?"—was borrowed from Schuller, who back in 1955 asked basically the same thing of people. According to Warren, it was a good question to use in order to find out what needs were not being met by the church.[33]

## The Ties That Do Not Bind

Not until 1984/85 did Warren receive his first invitation to speak at Schuller's Institute for Successful Church Leadership. Warren's growing congregation was numbering only about 500 to 600 at the time and he was barely 30 years old. Nevertheless, he was invited to give his testimony. *That is all*. He was given a small honorarium (as were several other people who gave their testimonies) and was sent on his way. During our interview, Warren explained, "I thought to myself, *Sure, okay, I don't mind giving my testimony somewhere.* I was excited to get the word out."

In the years that followed he was booked only twice more to speak at the Institute. He did not preach, did not speak in the Crystal Cathedral during weekend services, and did not meet Schuller. Finally, once Saddleback had grown rather large, Warren was invited to share *his testimony* yet again—this time in the cathedral itself—with Kay telling her part of the tale.

This 1991 event marked the first and only time Warren has spoken in the cathedral. Much to his credit, Schuller warmly received Rick and Kay and encouraged them to pursue their vision. In fact, the veteran pastor was very supportive of Warren and offered whatever help he might be able to give him, including his prayers. The mutual respect these two men shared for each other eventually led to many friendly exchanges and best wishes for each other.

But by the late 1990s, Warren had begun to notice that something was amiss at Schuller's church. As he told me, "I got a bunch of information about him, and then I also started seeing him have all kinds of nonbelievers speaking at his church." Then, Schuller had bestselling author Stephen Covey—a Mormon—speak at his church. This shocked Warren: "I thought, *This isn't right. How am I supposed to explain to all the ex-Mormons in my congregation why in the world Schuller has a Mormon up there talking?*"

### Making the Break

In response to Schuller's apparent pluralism, on March 13, 1998, Warren sent a letter to Chet Tolson of Schuller's Churches

Uniting in Global Mission (CUGM): "I must resign from the CUGM Council, I am afraid that the Crystal Cathedral's ministry is going in a very different direction than Saddleback Church." Warren added an explicit condemnation of Covey:

> I was deeply disappointed to see that the well-known Mormon speaker, Stephen Covey, was invited to speak at the Crystal Cathedral....[H]e is a devout and avowed Mormon who has publicly ridiculed evangelicals for faith in Christ alone in printed Mormon materials and in lectures to Mormons. Inviting Mr. Covey to preach, or even share a testimony, sends all the wrong signals and is very confusing to Christians who understand the differences between Mormonism and true salvation. Because Bob has chosen to associate with, and even provide a platform for, people who oppose historic Christianity and its doctrines, I feel, and my church feels, that I can no longer associate with CUGM. Please have my name removed from the letterhead of CUGM stationery.

Warren followed up this letter with another communication, dated September 15, 1998, to Glen DeMaster (Executive Pastor of the Crystal Cathedral). This was written because he continued to receive unsolicited mail from CUGM. He wrote, "I have resigned from the CUGM Council and have asked to have my name removed from the letterhead....Please remove my name from the mailing list for updates."

Needless to say, Schuller was not pleased. He wrote to Warren on September 25 of that year, expressing his dismay and disbelief about Covey ridiculing evangelicals. Schuller went so far as to say that Covey, despite his Mormonism, had professed Christ as Lord and Savior. So he did not see a problem. But in deference to Warren, Schuller asked for documentation proving the charges Warren had made.

He obliged Schuller with a package sent on January 29, 1999. It contained 1) an article from the *Baptist Press* titled "HMB Worker Uncovers Mormonism in Stephen Covey's '7 Habits'"; 2) a statement by Bill Gordon (Interfaith Witness Department, Home Missions Board, Southern Baptist Convention) documenting Covey's disparaging remarks about evangelicals; and 3) a cover letter to Schuller. This letter was only five sentences long and ended, "I'm enclosing the article that talks about Covey's view of evangelicals, and his view of the nature of Christ. I hope this clears things up."

## *The Rest of the Story*

Throughout 1999 there were several e-mails and letters exchanged between Warren and Schuller. These included a handwritten note by Warren in which he chided Schuller for "causing confusion" in the body of Christ. And when Schuller told Warren that the Muslim whom he had speak at the Crystal Cathedral worshiped the same God that "we" worshiped, Warren responded bluntly, "No, we don't!"

The break was complete—at least in Warren's mind. Schuller, however, kept seeking some form of reconciliation, either by way of a luncheon or another kind of get-together, including perhaps more appearances by Warren at his church. But all such offers were rebuffed. Still, Schuller did not give up, which is understandable given the fact that Warren's visibility and influence were steadily growing.

So in a letter on November 1, 2000, Schuller invited Warren to speak at his 2002 Institute gathering. Warren refused. Then, in a letter on April 26, 2002, Schuller asked Warren to be the *featured* speaker at his 2003 Institute conference. Warren, however, rejected the offer. As recently as April 28, 2004, Schuller implored Warren to speak at his Thirty-fifth Annual Institute event in January 2005. Warren, for a third time, said no.

### *Where's the Truth?*

Unfortunately, Schuller has not gone out of his way to make any of this known to the public, especially in light of the success of *The Purpose-Driven Life* and the unprecedented publicity surrounding it, Ashley Smith, and her captor, Brian Nichols (see introduction). On April 4, 2004, for instance, Schuller declared, "And there's Rick Warren, a pastor who today is phenomenal. He came to our institute time after time....And today Rick Warren is blessing millions of people."[34] Then, on March 14, 2005, during *Larry King Live,* when he was heralded as the man who "mentored" Rick Warren, he made no attempt to correct the misperception.

It is no wonder that rumors and gossip abound regarding the connection between the two men. Sometimes complete fabrications have been touted as absolute truth—especially on the Internet. One Web site boldly warns that "Warren recently [2004] held a conference with Robert Schuller" and that "Warren and Bill Hybels [senior pastor of Willow Creek Church] had a conference with Robert Schuller and Paul Crouch, among others, in January 2004."[35]

But no such event ever took place. Schuller's January 2004 conference was not attended by Rick Warren. The only January 2004 conference-like gathering at which Warren appeared was held in his own church—a pastor's premiere of Mel Gibson's *The Passion of the Christ.* And neither Bill Hybels nor Paul Crouch was there (nor was Robert Schuller). Hybels, in fact, was having his own *Passion* premiere all the way back in Chicago.

But enough about Warren and Schuller. The facts have been set forth. There are other issues to be explored and more questions to be answered as we proceed into our final chapter on Rick Warren and the purpose that drives him.

# CHAPTER 6

# Exaltation of Self?

*We've all known people who never grew up and never considered anything but their own wishes, desires, and cravings. Self-centeredness is the root of practically every problem—both personally and globally.*

RICK WARREN, *BETTER TOGETHER:*
*WHAT ON EARTH ARE WE HERE FOR?*

According to Warren, there is no *true* fulfillment to be found in pursuing one's own temporal and selfish purposes (wealth, fame, sex). There is no true fulfillment in trying to shape our own destiny or make up our own god. Instead, says Warren, we must turn to God and live out *His* purposes, gladly serving Him each day to build a heavenly storehouse of eternal riches. This is but a reflection of Jesus' lesson on storing up heavenly treasures as opposed to earthly treasures (Matthew 6:19-21).

Nonetheless, concerns have been raised that the purpose-driven concepts are centered around human self-empowerment, not God and His purposes for us. Further, Warren has been accused of focusing his ministry on himself, and has been called a "shameless marketeer and holy huckster," a "deceiver who willfully defrauds," a New Ager, and an occultist—not to mention a "money-grabbing preacher not interested in the truth of Scripture."[1] What, if any, truth is there in these allegations?

## ALL ABOUT ME

*Warren—instead of Scripture?* "Warren puts a lot of emphasis on the *importance* of his materials..., [saying,] 'The *last* thing many believers need today is to go to another Bible study.'...A little later in the same book he writes: 'I *strongly* urge you to gather a small group of friends and form a Purpose-Driven Life Reading Group.' "[2]

*The response.* These two quotes from *The Purpose-Driven Life* are 76 pages apart and have nothing to do with each other. The first quote is followed by an explanation: "They already know far more than they are putting into practice."[3] The point is, too many believers are doing little more than *hearing* the Word. They are not being "doers" of the Word (James 1:22). Interestingly, there is a readily accessible Internet-posted interview with Warren wherein he responds directly to a question about this comment:

> *Interviewer:* "You say in the book that the last thing believers need is another Bible study. Pardon me?"
>
> *Rick Warren:* "It takes more than Bible study to grow spiritual health. That's just one of the things. People

need Bible study experiences, but they also need worship experiences. They also need fellowship experiences. And they certainly need ministry experiences and mission experiences where they give out what they already know. Most people just take in and take in and take in, and we already know more than we're doing. We hear three or four messages a week, or Bible studies a week. We're using the radio and personal quiet time and Sunday school, and you get all this intake, and before you can apply it you're moving on to the next truth, assuming that because you took notes on it you've assimilated it. So what I really mean by that is simply what James said."[4]

As for the second quote, it is encouraging people to talk about Warren's book and not let the opportunity for spiritual growth pass them by. Prior to that statement, Warren even reminds readers that the real purpose of his book is only to let them know they need to 1) love God with all of their heart, 2) love their neighbor, 3) go make disciples, 4) baptize converts, and 5) teach new believers to follow Jesus' commandments.[5]

Warren is not eschewing Bible and doctrinal studies, but seeking to put them in their proper place. This is nothing new. Consider the words of A.W. Tozer, who is still revered as a noncompromising believer. He said, "The Spirit-filled walk demands that we live in the Word of God as a fish lives in the sea. By this I do not mean that we study the Bible merely, nor that we take a 'course' in Bible doctrine."[6]

Tozer was downplaying any overemphasis on intellectual "study" and an ungodly obsession with "doctrine" at the expense of life application and the manifestation of personal growth through being a doer of God's Word. As he also said, "Unused truth becomes as useless as an unused muscle."[7] This was Warren's point.

*Magic words?* Warren endorses prayer mantras verging on "vain repetitions" that he calls "breath prayers."[8]

*The response.* Actually, what Warren endorses in his book are short phrases speakable in a single breath: "You are with me." "I receive Your grace." "You are my God." A person is supposed to think about what these words mean during the day. It is a way of being in constant prayer—little reminders that God is near, that He loves you, and that you are to live for Him. They are not "vain repetitions," which Warren condemns: "Jesus called thoughtless worship 'vain repetitions.'"[9]

Indeed, Christ denounced such false forms of worship in Matthew 6:7 as "much speaking" (or "babbling speech") uttered by Gentiles in a vain attempt to sway the will of their pagan gods. As *The Wycliffe Bible Commentary* explains, such prayers were an attempt "to overcome God's unwillingness to respond by wearying him with words."[10] Obviously, this has nothing to do with Warren's short phrases that help people keep their minds fixed on Jesus in the middle of their busy lives. They are not mantras.

*Man in place of God?* "Warren explains: 'The way you *see* your life *shapes* your life. How you define life determines your destiny....' This is blasphemy. Who is in control? Would Rick Warren have us believe that we are the masters of our own destiny? Dare he elevate man to the place of God? That is exactly what he is doing."[11]

***The response.*** First, in the dedication of *The Purpose-Driven Life,* Warren points to God's sovereignty, foreknowledge, and predestination. He is saying that the Christian God is in control, that nothing surprises Him, and that it is no "accident" readers have a book about Him. For those who accept Christ, their reading of the book was the Spirit leading and guiding them to salvation. In fact, right after Warren says his book is "no accident," he cites Ephesians 1:11, which is about the inheritance Christians are predestined to receive from God.

Second, as for Warren's "shapes your life" quote, it is not a swipe at God's sovereignty. Nor is Warren saying we should put ourselves in "the place of God." The very title of the chapter these words are found in is "Seeing Life from God's View." He is contrasting how different perspectives determine how we live. Adopting a godly perspective (an eternal one) will produce godly decisions, eternal treasure, and a life that glorifies Jesus Christ. But looking at life from a human perspective (a sinful one) will only produce sinful decisions, worldly gain, and fleeting pleasure that is worthless. As he says, "Your perspective will influence how you invest your time, spend your money, use your talents, and value your relationships."[12]

Saddleback Church is firmly grounded in the long-held Christian concept that God alone is in control of our lives and the world. Through wars, persecution, sickness, financial difficulties, loneliness, anguish, fear, and suffering—He is sovereign. "God's in control," Warren affirms. "If I didn't know that fact, I would be very frightened....Society is declining in its moral decay. But God is still in control....You're free to make choices in your life. But you are not totally free. God is in control."[13]

When it comes to human destiny, each of the pastors at Saddleback teaches what Warren expressed so well in his 2002 article "It All Starts with God." He noted, "It is only in God that we discover our origin, our identity, our meaning, our purpose, our significance, and *our destiny*. Every other path leads to a dead end."[14]

## Doing Church and Getting Saved

*Gimmicky church practices?* "Having a successful church ultimately depends on God, not man. Warren, however, follows the manipulative [Peter] Drucker model and likes to use certain gimmicks....[Warren says,] 'The difference between an average service and an outstanding service is flow.' Sorry, the difference between an average service and an outstanding one is the manifest presence of God."[15]

*The response.* In *The Purpose-Driven Church,* under the heading "Measuring Success," Warren writes, "Successful ministry is 'building the church on the purposes of God, in the power of the Holy Spirit, and *expecting* the results from God.'" As for "gimmicks," he declares: "Strong churches are not built on programs, personalities, or gimmicks. They are built on the eternal purposes of God."[16] In regard to the "flow" of a service, it is not a gimmick. Nor does it have anything to do with the "manifest presence of God" (or a lack of it). God is *already* manifest wherever Christians are by the power and presence of the Holy Ghost. Jesus promised, "I am with you *alway[s]*" (Matthew 28:20).

*Warren's Ways*

In context, Warren is making a sensible observation about things that might distract unbelievers: unnecessarily long prayers, lengthy offerings, uncomfortable gaps of silence between speakers, apparent confusion by leaders about what comes next, and a service length that visiting non-Christians cannot handle thanks to their shortened "attention span" in this age of sound clips, MTV, network news briefs, and commercials.[17] In other words, we must be considerate to visitors.

Church leaders, for instance, already know that the air conditioning should be turned on *before* guests arrive. And what about setting up chairs for attendees (as opposed to having people set up their own)? Should not programs be handed out? Is there not supposed to be an orderly manner in which to take communion, or should everyone just run up at once to a table of bread and wine to grab what they can?

These aspects of a church experience are not "gimmicks," nor do they discount the value of God's manifest presence in the congregation. They relate to widely recognized parts of service preparation and execution that must be taken care of. In *The Purpose-Driven Church,* Warren merely adds to this list a number of other things that can be done to make a service even better—*outstanding* as opposed to *average.*[18]

*Drucker's Doings*

As for Peter Drucker (born 1909), he is no enemy of religion, especially Christianity. He accepts biblical standards of morality and ethics, eschews liberalism, appreciates church work, is staunchly anti-Communist, and "is cynical of big government."[17] He has gone so far as to defend religious ideals and freedoms such as "school prayer," and he greatly compliments the value of Christianity as a solution to the ills of society.[19]

According to *Christianity Today,* he "gladly stresses the church's spiritual mission, but he notes that churches also have a societal role....He told *Forbes* that pastoral megachurches are 'surely the most important social phenomenon in American society in the last thirty years.' "[20]

His teachings revolve entirely around business management, leadership, politics, government, and social issues. And they seem to be, in general, fairly nonoffensive: "Stop thinking about what you can achieve; think about what you can contribute"; "Ask what needs to be done"; "Develop action plans"; "Take responsibility"; "Focus on opportunities instead of challenges"; "The objective of any organization is to positively change the lives of those with whom it has direct contact....The mark of a successful organization is the elevated competence of those with whom it has direct contact."[21]

Drucker, as a professing Christian, has a healthy respect for God's Word. In fact, during a 2003 interview he stated that the absolute, hands-down best texts on leadership remain "the Epistles of St. Paul"! Also noteworthy is Drucker's ongoing admiration for the church, which he believes is undergoing a renaissance.[22] In his *Landmarks of Tomorrow,* Drucker—a nontheologian—even points people to God:

> The individual needs [a] return to spiritual values, for he can survive in the present human situation only by reaffirming that man is not just a biological and psychological being but also a spiritual being, that is, creature, and existing for the purposes of his Creator and subject to Him.[23]

Clearly, the Drucker–Warren connection is nothing more than an internationally recognized expert in "leadership" giving advice about leadership to a leader. And, according to Drucker himself, the Bible is his number-one leadership text. He is not a theologian, a spiritual mentor, or any kind of religious leader.

> ***Corporate salvation?*** Warren "has been heavily influenced" by business guru Peter Drucker. And like Drucker, Warren believes that the *real* answer to humanity's problems is something called "Communitarianism"—a means of forming "community" wherein man can perfect himself through an evolutionary process linked to the creation of a better society. "The solution for both authors is not salvation in its personal sense."[24]

***The response.*** As previously touched on, Rick Warren enjoys a close relationship with Peter Drucker, the renowned writer, lecturer, and thinker who specializes in leadership. He has for years mentored Warren in the area of leadership management. This has given rise to all kinds of speculation about Drucker, Warren, and an alleged agenda they both have to transform the world's churches and society into some kind of New Age utopia. But their association has a far less sinister aim.

*Drucker and Christ*

Warren first met Peter Drucker some 20 years ago. He sought out the celebrated expert on leadership because he wanted advice on how to run a large organization (specifically, a church). Drucker's management principles are basic to good leadership: figure out what needs to be done; evaluate your performance; be willing to let go of what is not working; think internationally; use technology; prioritize tasks; use your strengths; move forward cautiously; continue developing your character.[25]

These observations easily line up with biblical truths about being wise, thoughtful, hardworking, and diligent. Yet the two men's link has raised concerns. Why? Because Drucker is supposedly a "humanist," and "humanism" in its varied forms is in general anti-Christian.

However, Drucker is actually an avowed Christian, as we noted earlier. And no hard evidence has ever been presented to show otherwise. He has never labeled himself as either a secular or religious humanist in the usual, pejorative sense. And in those instances when he has made positive comments about certain aspects of humanism, he has balanced them with criticisms of humanism as a system. For example, several decades ago he wrote that, although the humanist ethic might give some measure of "integrity, courage, and steadfastness," in the end it is a bankrupt worldview that leads only to despair because it "cannot give meaning—neither to life nor death."[26]

Drucker, as a confessing Christian, believes in personal salvation, rather than any kind of corporate salvation via the perfecting of mankind in a communitarian atmosphere. He has declared that "surely the collapse of Marxism as a creed signifies the end of the belief in salvation by society" and concludes, "The end of the belief in salvation by society surely marks an inward turning. It makes possible renewed emphasis on the individual, the person. It may even lead—at least we can so hope—to a return to individual responsibility."[27]

### According to America's Pastor

Warren, even more than Drucker, stresses *personal* salvation. In *The Purpose-Driven Life* we read, "God's Word is clear that you can't earn your salvation. It comes only by grace, not your effort....God loves you....The greatest expression of this is the sacrifice of God's Son for you." Warren then makes his beliefs clear: "The invitation to be part of God's family [also known as salvation] is universal, but there is one condition: faith in Jesus." And at Warren's pastors.com Web site, the "What We Believe" page reads, "We believe that for the salvation of lost and sinful people, regeneration by the Holy Spirit is absolutely essential."[28]

Transcripts of Warren's sermons show he has *always* taught personal salvation through faith in Jesus: "When Jesus died for your sins, which ones did He include? All of them!...Jesus gave His life and He paid the 'bill' of the penalty for our sins."[29] In other words, salvation is personal to Warren. It has nothing to do with any kind of evolutionary leap of humanity, Communitarianism, or building a better society.

Any of Warren's references to "community" refer to the joy and other benefits that come from being active in a Bible-based church. "Community" at Saddleback and throughout the purpose driven network of churches is defined as "an uncommon commitment to spread the Good News of Jesus Christ, an uncommon dedication to see lives changed, an uncommon vision of thriving, growing churches, and an uncommon zeal for the global glory of God."[30] As Martha Stewart would say, "It's a good thing."

With regard to the betterment of society, Warren's only thoughts on this issue are grounded solely in God's many commands to assist the poor (Acts 20:35; 1 John 3:17), feed and clothe the needy (James 2:15-16), comfort orphans and widows (Galatians 2:10; 1 Timothy 5:16; James 1:27), and "love thy neighbor" (Matthew 22:39).*

## JUST TO MAKE YOU HAPPY

*Misrepresenting God?* In *The Purpose-Driven Life,* Warren says love is the essence of God's character. But "the essence of God is not love alone. While our God is a

---

* See Warren's comments on this issue on pages 24–27 of the interview.

loving, merciful God, this is not the extent of His being. God has every emotion, including one that in our day has been de-popularized: hate."[31]

*The response.* First, God does not possess "every emotion." He does not feel awe because He is perfectly awesome in Himself. He is never surprised because He knows all things. He never feels embarrassed, vulnerable, afraid, covetous, guilty, or prideful. Second, when Warren says God is love (1 John 4:8), then declares that love is the "essence" of His character, he nowhere suggests that love is "the extent" of God's being. In the passage from which the above quote is taken, Warren explains, "There is perfect love in the fellowship of the Trinity."[32]

This has nothing to do with stressing God's "love" at the expense of His "hate" (or wrath). Warren is repeating a standard Christian observation about "love" within the Godhead (hence, God *is* love). Millard J. Erickson, a distinguished professor of theology who has served at several Christian universities and seminaries, addressed this issue in *God in Three Persons* when he pointed out that the "God is Love" declaration reaches to the very core of God's triune nature. It means far more "than merely, 'God is loving.'" Or, as Warren says in his book, "It doesn't say God *has* love. He *is* love!"[33]

Third, nowhere does Warren discount God's other emotions, attributes, qualities, or characteristics, including "hate" (or wrath). He simply does not mention them in the passage in question because they are not the subjects at hand. Rather, the topic there is God's love for His people as seen in Ephesians 1:4-5. Warren does mention God's wrath later in the book: "The Bible warns unbelievers [non-Christians], *'He will pour out his anger and wrath on those who live for themselves'* [that is to say, continue to live as non-Christians]."[34]

> **Pleasing God in the wrong way?** Warren says "all you have to do to earn smiles, friendship and heavenly rewards from God is do what Jesus did....[But if] all I have to do is what Jesus did, then that means I have to be perfect."...
>
> But then Warren says, "He knows you are incapable of being perfect....What God looks at is the attitude of your heart." Is God "all about sincerity"?
>
> In sum, Warren falsely teaches that our good works and godly choices can please God and make Him smile. But what pleases God "is Jesus—His life of perfect obedience lived for sinners."[35]

*The response.* This concern misrepresents Warren in two ways. First, it distorts his heartfelt (and biblical) position on obedience. Second, it condemns his sincere efforts to be balanced by 1) simply encouraging readers to be like Christ (through obedience), and 2) telling them God understands when they fail.[36]

The concern misses Warren's obvious points: 1) God wants obedience—as Jesus said, "If ye love me, keep my commandments" (John 14:15); and 2) as much as we seek to emulate Christ, we are imperfect, so *when* (not if) we blow it, God understands because He sees beyond our failures into our hearts, where our true motives and intentions reside (1 Chronicles 28:9; Psalm 94:11; 139:1-6).

Further, God does indeed take pleasure in what His followers do in His name and for His glory. King David, for example, after offering his gifts for the building of the temple, prayed, "I know also, my God, that thou triest the heart, and hast pleasure in uprightness" (1 Chronicles 29:17). God is indeed pleased with our good works, deeds, choices, and attitudes because they glorify Him (John 15:8).

Regarding heavenly rewards, this is a long-established Christian doctrine based on 1 Corinthians 3:11-15, where Paul speaks of believers being rewarded for their "work." And as Revelation 14:13 says of those who die in Christ, their "works do follow them."

*New Age word play?* "Warren quotes 2 Chronicles 14:4 (MSG), which says: '*Center* their lives in GOD'; and Philippians 4:7 (MSG): 'Christ displaces worry at the *center* of your life.'... Centering is a New Age concept."[37]

*The response.* In context, Warren's topic is putting *Jesus* at the center of your life. He asks, "Who are you going to live for? What are you going to build your life around?" and then adds, "None is strong enough to hold you together when life starts breaking apart. You need an unshakable center."[38] This reflects the great truth of Matthew 7:24-27 about building our lives on Christ.

To link a single word such as "center" to something like New Age "centering" and then use that term to tie Warren into the New Age simply doesn't follow. This line of reasoning has no justification and can be used to condemn anything or anyone (see endnote 39).[39]

## THE SEEKER-SENSITIVE ISSUE

*Church or entertainment?* In seeker-sensitive services biblical sermons "are often replaced with short talks, videos, and skits—anything that the audience will find more enjoyable and entertaining.[40]

***The response.*** At Saddleback Church the weekly sermon is never replaced by anything. There is always a straightforward 45- to 60-minute sermon. On some weekends scattered throughout the year, this sermon is punctuated by one to three short videos, testimonies, skits (two to five minutes each), or a combination of these, which illustrate the main points of the sermon.

***Warren wants wealth?*** Warren and others "try to teach us that being a community of faithful purpose means that we peddle our gospel of wealth and prosperity."[41]

***The response.*** *The Purpose-Driven Life* declares:[42]

- "Wealth can be lost instantly....Real security can only be found in that which can never be taken from you—your relationship to God."

- "It is a fatal mistake to assume that God's goal for your life is material prosperity or popular success....The abundant life has nothing to do with *material* abundance, and faithfulness to God does not guarantee success in a career or even in ministry."

- "Many believers have abandoned living for God's great purposes and settled for personal fulfillment and emotional stability. That is narcissism, not discipleship. Jesus did not die on the cross just so we could live comfortable, well-adjusted lives....He wants to make us like himself before he takes us to heaven."

- "Wealth is certainly not a sin, but failing to use it for God's glory is. Servants of God are always more concerned about ministry than money."

*Deleting the cross?* "The word of the cross by Paul (1 Corinthians 1:18), is not being preached in these churches that have adopted the 'user-friendly' model."[43]

*The response.* *The Purpose-Driven Life* says much that addresses this concern:[44]

- "God has chosen you to have a relationship with Jesus, who died on the cross for you."
- "If you want to know how much you matter to God, look at Christ with his arms outstretched on the cross."
- "When he paid for our sins on the cross, the veil in the temple that symbolized our separation from God was split from top to bottom."
- "In the Old Testament, God took pleasure in the many sacrifices of worship because they foretold of Jesus' sacrifice for us on the cross."
- "[Praise God] for what Jesus did for you on the cross. *God's Son died for you!*"
- "The church is so significant that Jesus died on the cross for it."
- "[Jesus] was willing to die a shameful death on the cross because of the joy he knew would be his afterwards."
- "[God] wants his lost children found!...[T]he Cross proves that."

- "When Jesus stretched his arms out wide on the cross, he was saying, 'I love you *this* much!'....Whenever you feel apathetic about your mission in the world, spend some time thinking about what Jesus did for you on the cross."

Some critics, though, have alleged there is "no Gospel at all" to be found either at Saddleback's seeker services or in Warren's book. "It's the Gospel without the bad news. People are coming to have purpose in their lives, but they are not coming to get saved from sin."[45]

However, *The Purpose-Driven Life* includes several key Gospel words in numerous places: *sin* (45 times), *sins* (14 times), and *sinners* (6 times). In one passage, for instance, we read, "Sacrifice is the essence of love. Jesus modeled this: *'Be full of love for others, following the example of Christ who loved you and gave Himself to God as a sacrifice to take away your sins.'*" And Warren's sermons are packed with warnings about sin and its consequence—hell (the "bad news"):

> If you choose to be separate from God *now,* you will choose to be separated from God for *eternity,* and that is called "Hell." You say, "Rick, is there a real hell? Is hell a real place?" Well, of course there is. Jesus talked about it. Some people say: "Well, I don't believe in hell." Well, that doesn't make it not real.[46]

Such teachings at Saddleback stretch over many years. For instance, in 1992 pastor Tom Holladay taught, "Either—we suffer separation in hell. Or—we enjoy celebration in heaven. That's the greatest good news ever. That's also the greatest bad news ever....Whether we believe in it or not—it's real. We will either suffer separation or enjoy celebration."[47]

As recently as Easter 2004, Warren affirmed this again—in a few words that capture the heart of both the man and his message:

> You were created to last forever. And you're going to live forever in one of two places—heaven or hell. God says...*I've done everything possible to get you into heaven including send My Son to die for you.* To go to hell you have to reject the love of God. Why would anybody do that?[48]

# Rick Warren and His Message

Long ago A.W. Tozer observed, "Christianity is rarely found pure....The truth is so vast and mighty that no one is capable of taking it all in....It requires the whole company of ransomed souls properly to reflect the whole body of revealed truth." And in *The Christ in the Bible Commentary* by A.B. Simpson (1844–1919) we read, "No single doctrinal principle is important enough to displace the Lord Jesus Christ Himself as the one name that alone should dominate His Church."

Like Tozer and Simpson, Rick Warren has learned that what matters most is not denominations, pet doctrines, and philosophical musings that have no practical value to the average person bound for hell. Consequently, getting people away from *religion* and into a *relationship* with Jesus (the Jesus of the Bible) is

Warren's all-consuming passion—and it is a passion of just about everyone I know at Saddleback Church.

I wrote this book to tell Rick Warren's story and to examine some of the most serious accusations that have been made against his faith, ministry, and church. But I've received far more than I bargained for, which seems to be God's way of doing things.

By looking more closely at how others have been spiritually gifted in my home church, I've received a better understanding of exactly how God has gifted me for service. And after learning more details about the route God has taken Warren in life, I've come to see that wherever and however we may currently be serving God has no bearing whatsoever on where or how He may want us to serve Him in the future. Finally, my reading through literally hundreds of Warren's sermons has given me a far deeper appreciation for the magnitude of need the world presents to Christians.

So my own endeavors will now be heading in a different direction, one I think will be more in line with God's purposes for me—while, ironically, being far less me-centered. And I have decided to give more to charity, hoping to be a Christian who demonstrates his faith by being as interested in the helpless and hopeless as Jesus was.

My prayer is that readers have learned a few things, too: 1) The Gospel must always be preached, 2) the truth must never be compromised, and 3) the Scriptures must be upheld. At the same time, however, I hope that another message has come through these pages: Things are not always as they appear to be in the rough-and-tumble world of religion, especially in the area of apologetics (that is to say, defending the faith).

It is true that Christians are commanded to contend for the faith (Jude 3), preserve the purity of the Gospel (Galatians 1:6-9; 1 Peter 3:15), test all things to find what is good (1 Thessalonians 5:21), and even correct those who are in error (2 Timothy 4:2). But these sacred directives can quickly devolve into unholy traps set by forces of darkness when people end up being falsely accused (Exodus 20:16; Matthew 19:18).

In conclusion, I can only say that Warren, from all of the documentation I have been able to acquire and analyze, is a biblically sound Christian. And *The Purpose-Driven Life* is an invaluable resource that has been, and undoubtedly will continue to be, used to lead many people to the one true God of the Bible. It presents to a lost and dying world the hope of new life in the arms of a loving God, whose existence gives all of us purpose and meaning. As Warren himself has said countless times, "It's all about God." I couldn't agree more—to God be the glory, to God be the praise.

# Notes

## Introduction: That Old-Time Religion

1. Rick Warren, *The Purpose-Driven Life* (Grand Rapids, MI: Zondervan, 2002), pp. 7-8.

2. "A Place to Draw Nearer to God," *The Manna*, May 2004, online at www.wolc .org; Paul Harris, "How One Man's Gospel Tale Became a Global Bestseller," *The Observer*, July 11, 2004.

3. Mark Kelly, "P.E.A.C.E. Plan a Worldwide Revolution, Warren Tells Angel Stadium Crowd," April 19, 2005, online at purposedriven.com.

4. Ashley Smith, News Conference, March 13, 2005. All Smith and Nichols quotes (as related by Smith) are taken from this press conference.

5. Warren, p. 257.

6. For biblical passages relating to the following numbered points, see Genesis 1:1; John 1:1; Isaiah 45:12; Malachi 2:10; Acts 17:24-28; Romans 3:23; John 3:16; Romans 14:17 (and 15:13); Galatians 5:22-23; Titus 1:16; and Ecclesiastes 9:10; 12:13.

7. See Psalm 39:4-5.

8. Ephesians 2:10.

9. For biblical passages relating to the following bullet points, see Romans 5:3; 2 Corinthians 6:10 (and 7:4); James 1:2; Romans 12:4-8; Job 10:8 (and 31:15); Psalm 11:3 (and 139:14); Zechariah 12:1; Isaiah 64:8; Matthew 6:25-34; Romans 12:3; Philippians 3:20-21; James 4:4,9; Matthew 16:23; Mark 12:33; Colossians 3:2; Hebrews 12:1-2; Deuteronomy 12:18; Philippians 4:4; 1 Thessalonians 5:16; 2 Timothy 2:4,24; Titus 2:12; Ephesians 5:1-2; and James 1:27.

10. These two accusations appear in many places—e.g., **heresy** (Richard Bennett, "The Purpose Driven Life: Demanding the Very Nature of God," part 2, online at monergism.com, and Frances Swaggart, "Tolerance at the Expense of Truth," *The Evangelist*, Mar. 2005, p. 15); and **poison** (Will Weedon, *Issues, Etc.*, radio broad-

cast interview, KFUO, Oct. 29, 2003 [Weedon is senior pastor of St. Paul Lutheran Church of Hamel, Illinois]).

Similar remarks may be found in *What You Need to Know About the Purpose-Driven Church* (Bethany, OK: Southwest Radio Bible Church, 2004) by Larry Spargimino, who implies that Warren and others within the church-growth movement are "lunatics" (p. 10).

11. See Andre Bustanoby, "Spirit-led or Purpose-Driven?" withchrist.org/purpose.htm, and Bennett, online at www.monergism.com; Standing in the Gap Ministries, "Here Are Some Observations," www.antiosas.org/Warren1.htm; Smith, p. 8; and Spargimino, p. 9.

Equally harsh condemnations may be found in Robert Jenkins, "Rick Warren and Bill Hybels: Men of God or Dangerous Hucksters?" online at www.observations.net; Richard Bennett, "The Adulation of Man in The Purpose-Driven Life," online at www.monergism.com; Mac Dominick, *Rebuilding the Tower of Babel* (Lexington, SC: Cutting Edge Ministries, 2005); Todd Friel, "Uh-Oh. The Purpose-Driven Problem," online at www.mcchronicle.com; James Sundquist, *Who's Driving the Purpose-Driven Church?* (Bethany, OK: Rock Salt Publishing, 2004), pp. 15-16 (Sundquist actually applies to Warren 1 Timothy 4:1, which warns believers about those who in the last days "shall depart from the faith, giving heed to seducing spirits, and doctrines of devils"); and Paul Proctor, "It's Your Choice," Mar 11, 2005, online at newswithviews.com.

## An Interview: Rick Warren in His Own Words

1. These statements regarding Blanchard directly contradict the many baseless rumors, bits of misinformation, and accusations alleging some kind of close link between Warren, Blanchard, and the false beliefs that have been advanced by various persons whom Blanchard has unwisely associated himself with via several different avenues. For example, Blanchard wrote endorsements for New Ager Deepak Chopra's *Seven Spiritual Laws of Success* (1995) as well for *The 11th Element* (2003) by the influential New Ager Robert Scheinfeld. Blanchard also penned forewords to *Death and Letting Go* (2003) by New Ager/clairvoyant Ellen Tadd; *Mind Like Water* (2002) by New Age proponent Jim Ballard; and *What Would Buddha Do at Work?* (2001) by celebrated advocate of Buddhism Franz Metcalf.

Recently, however, Blanchard has been made aware of the problem with these materials and has sought to deepen his understanding of not only Christian doctrine, but also the issues that are causing controversy and concern among Christians. I personally contacted the leadership of Blanchard's "Lead Like Jesus" organization in mid-May 2005, and at that time I began helping them draft a public statement addressing these sensitive issues. Then, in a May 24, 2005, e-mail to me, the Lead Like Jesus president—Phyllis Hendry—assured me that Blanchard was not seeking to endorse *any* non-Christian beliefs by lending his name to various books. Instead, he had been a victim of lack of knowledge concerning the full consequences of what various non-Christians were believing and teaching—and as a result fell prey to those who wanted to use his name and celebrity status to help them. Efforts to assist Blanchard are ongoing.

It also must be noted here that contrary to rumors, Blanchard has *never* (as of mid-2005) spoken at Saddleback or taken part in any training of Saddleback pastors, church members, other church pastors, or church workers. A November 2003 video clip often cited by Warren's critics as proof of his ties to Blanchard (see www.saddlebackfamily.com/peace/Services/110203_high.asx) actually shows nothing more than Blanchard expressing his support for Warren's P.E.A.C.E. Plan. And Warren's statement in the video about Blanchard signing up to "help" train people only has to do with Blanchard's willingness to offer insights about the best ways to implement Warren's ideas from a *business* perspective, which happens to be Blanchard's field of expertise.

## Chapter 1: Here I Am, Lord

1. Materials used to construct this synopsis of Warren's life (c. 1954–1979) include the following interviews, sermons, and articles: Dot Warren, testimony given during "The Truth About Change" (a Rick Warren sermon), part 4, Sept. 11, 1994; Chaundel Holladay, author's interview, April 25, 2005; Rick Warren, "What's a Family For?" part 1, May 22, 1988; "What's a Family For?" part 4, May 14, 1995; Memorial Service for Jimmy Warren, April 30, 1999; Rick Warren, "What Would I Do Differently Now That I Know What I Know That I Know?" Jan. 2004; Rick Warren, "All in the Family," part 3, Apr. 1987; Rick Warren, "How God Talks to You," Feb. 16, 1992; Ted Parks and Tim Stafford, "The Shockingly Ordinary Purpose-Driven Life of Rick Warren," *Christianity Today,* Nov./Dec. 2003, online at www.christianitytoday.com; William Lobdell, "Pastor with a Purpose," *Los Angeles Times,* Sept. 29, 2003, online at www.latimes.com; Rick Warren, "How to Communicate to Change Lives" (PDC Conference), part 1, session 3, 1997; Rick Warren, "W.A. Criswell's Legacy to Extend for Generations," *MinistryToolBox,* Jan. 23, 2002, issue #36, online at pastors.com; Rick Warren, "Compatibility: Choosing the Right Partner," part 4, Jan. 27, 2001; Jim Hinch, "Pastor: a Man on a Mission," *Orange County Register,* May 25, 2003, online at www.ocregister.com; Tim Stafford, "A Regular Purpose-Driven Guy," *Christianity Today,* Nov. 18, 2002, online at www.ctlibrary.com; "Don't Let Your Doubts Defeat You!" part 2, Aug. 3, 1986; Rick Warren, "How to Recognize God's Voice," part 4, Mar. 1, 1992; Kay Warren, "Understanding Your Husband's Deepest Needs," part 7, May 13, 1990; Rick Warren, "Six Secrets of a Satisfying Marriage," part 1, April 22, 1995; Rick Warren, "Defusing Fears in Relationships," part 5, May 21, 1995; Rick Warren, "How to Handle Life's Hurts," part 1, Nov. 10, 1985; Rick Warren, "How to Communicate to Change Lives" (PDC Conference), part 2, 1997.

## Chapter 2: Driven by Purpose—Directed by God

1. Materials used to construct this synopsis of Warren's life (c. 1979–2005) include the following interviews, sermons, and articles: Chaundel Holladay, author's interview, April 25, 2005; Rick Warren, "Targeting Your Community" (PDC

Conference), session 2, 1997; *Saddleback Church: 25 Years of Changing Lives Together* (Lake Forest, CA: Saddleback Church and Rick Warren, 2005); Rick Warren, "God Uses Weak People," *Leadership Lifter,* n.d.; William Lobdell, "Pastor with a Purpose," *Los Angeles Times,* Sept. 29, 2003, online at www.la times.com; Rick Warren, "Discovering Church Membership," C.L.A.S.S. 101; Rick Warren, "What It Means to Have Faith," part 1, Mar. 8, 1992; Rick Warren, "Why Hasn't God Answered My Prayer?" part 3, Feb. 22, 1987; Rick Warren, "How to Communicate to Change Lives" (PDC Conference), part 1, session 3; Rick Warren, "Attracting a Crowd" (PDC Conference), part 2, session 6 of 12, 1997; Rick Warren, "What Would I Do Differently Now That I Know What I Know That I Know?" Jan. 2004; Tim Stafford, "A Regular Purpose-Driven Guy," *Christianity Today,* Nov. 18, 2002, online at www.ctlibrary.com; Rick Warren, "W.A. Criswell's Legacy to Extend for Generations," *MinistryToolBox,* Jan. 23, 2002, issue #36, online at pastors.com.

## Chapter 3: Seekers and Saints

1. Rick Warren, in Michael Duduit, "Purpose-Driven Preaching: An Interview with Rick Warren," *MinistryToolBox,* Aug. 7, 2002, issue #62, online at www.pastors .com (endnote also applicable to the previous quote in main text).

2. Rick Warren, "The Purpose of Preaching" (The Pastors Gathering), part 2, n.d. (endnote also applicable to the next two quotes in main text).

3. Rick Warren, *The Purpose-Driven Life* (Grand Rapids, MI: Zondervan, 2002), pp. 53-58.

4. Rick Warren, "Discovering Church Membership," C.L.A.S.S. 101; Rick Warren, "God's Final Verdict," n.d.; and Rick Warren, "God's Passion for You," part 2, Feb. 28, 2004.

5. Warren, "Discovering."

6. Warren, *The Purpose-Driven Life,* p. 20.

7. "What CLASS Is," online at www.pastors.com. All descriptions that follow are taken from this document. C.L.A.S.S. is an acronym for Christian Life And Service Seminars.

8. *Saddleback Church: 25 Years of Changing Lives Together* (Lake Forest, CA: Saddleback Church and Rick Warren, 2005), p. 4.

9. Rick Warren, "Purpose-Driven Life" (PDC Conference), session 2, 2002.

10. Warren, *The Purpose-Driven Church* (Grand Rapids, MI: Zondervan, 1995), see chapter 3.

11. Warren, *The Purpose-Driven Church,* see chapter 7.

12. *Saddleback Church,* pp. 6-7.

13. Warren, "Purpose-Driven Life."

14. Rick Warren, interview on "The Purpose-Driven Life," *Newsnight* (CNN), Mar. 16, 2005.

15. Warren, *The Purpose-Driven Life,* pp. 7-8.

16. Bertrand Russell. Quoted in Warren, *The Purpose-Driven Life,* p. 17.

17. Rick Warren, "How to Communicate to Change Lives" (PDC Conference), part 1, session 3, 1997.

18. Leland Ryken, James C. Wilhoit, and Tremper Longman III, gen. eds., *Dictionary of Biblical Imagery* (Downers Grover, IL: InterVarsity Press, 1998), p. 465.

19. Warren, *The Purpose-Driven Life,* p. 43.

20. See William Lobdell, "Pastor with a Purpose," *Los Angeles Times,* Sept. 29, 2003, online at www.latimes.com.

21. Rick Warren has recounted this story many times. This is a compilation of three versions, each of which brought out complementary aspects of the episode.

## Chapter 4: A Watered-Down Christianity?

1. Nathan Busenitz, "A Sense of Purpose: Evaluating the Claims of the Purpose-Driven Life," online at www.gty.org. This review also appeared in *Fool's Gold* (Wheaton, IL: Crossway, 2004), edited by John MacArthur, the senior pastor of Grace Community Church and one of Warren's harshest and most vocal critics.

2. Busenitz. This is the substance of John MacArthur's criticisms of Rick Warren (cf. "John MacArthur on CNN's *NewsNight* with Aaron Brown," press release, Grace Community Church, online at www.gty.org).

3. In *The Purpose-Driven Life,* Warren mentions most of the topics listed by this critic, including self-denial (pp. 18-19, 53-58); God's law (pp. 90, 123, 129, 142, 187, 189); grace (pp. 72, 78, 86, 92); sin (pp. 78-79, 162); redemption (pp. 78-79, 86, 97, 288); and the cross (pp. 58, 79, 86, 105, 112, 132, 178, 198, 288, 294).

4. Busenitz. Busenitz is the director of the Shepherds' Fellowship (a system of churches linked to Grace Community Church) and an adjunct faculty member at The Master's College and Seminary.

5. Rick Warren, *The Purpose-Driven Life* (Grand Rapids, MI: Zondervan, 2002), pp. 232, 203-204.

6. Richard Bennett, "The Purpose-Driven Life: Demeaning the Very Nature of God," part 2, online at www.monergism.com.

7. Rick Warren, *The Purpose-Driven Life,* pp. 25, 117-118.

8. "God *yearns* to deal mercifully and kindly with us" (Howard Culbertson, professor of world evangelism, Southern Nazarene University, "Jonah, the Reluctant Missionary," http://home.snu.edu/~hculbert/jonah.htm); "God *yearns* for mankind to come to repentance!" (Wisconsin Evangelical Lutheran Synod, "Topical Q&A," online at www.sels.net); "God *yearns* to restore us to wholeness and life" (J. Nelson Kraybill, Associated Mennonite Biblical Seminary, "New Testament

Vision of a New Humanity," www.newlifeministries-nlm.org); "God *yearns* jealously over our spirits' (James 4:5). He *longs* to bless us!" (Raymond C. Ortlund Jr., First Presbyterian Church of Augusta, Georgia, "Psalm 51:17 and the Beauty of Brokenness," *Faith*, Nov. 4, 2001, online at www.firstpresaugusta.org).

9. Spargimino, p. 15. This criticism has been raised often (e.g., Brian Jonson, "An Examination of Rick Warren's Teaching on 'Exponential Growth,'" online at www.monergism.com). It has further been said, "If Warren is right about the unimportance of doctrine, 'then the Mormons should take great comfort'" (Spargimino, p. 15).

10. Rick Warren, *The Purpose-Driven Life*, p. 37.

11. Rick Warren, "Helping Your Members Mature Little by Little," *MinistryToolBox*, June, 30, 2004, issue #161, online at pastors.com. Bible references for Warren's view include Phil. 2:12-15; 2 Pet. 3:18; 1 Jn. 2:27; 2 Tim. 3:16; and 1 Pet. 2:2-3.

12. J. Gresham Machen, *The Virgin Birth of Christ* (Grand Rapids, MI: Baker Book House, 1930), pp. 395-396. Quoted in Walter Martin, *Essential Christianity* (Ventura, CA: Regal, 1980), p. 51. I am indebted to Steve Devore and Steve Lagoon of Christian Apologetics Ministries for finding not only this reference, but also the next citation (see Steve Devore and Steve Lagoon, "The Counter-Cult Salvation: A Look at the Deity of Christ for Salvation Issue," www.visi.com/~steved/cam/salvation.pdf).

13. "[Faith] must embrace the truth of the gospel and of Christ's redemptive work for us. But how much of the gospel must one know to be saved? This is not easy to say. We must have enough knowledge to realize that we are sinners who need redemption, that we cannot save ourselves but that only Christ can redeem us from sin and from the wrath of God, and that Christ died and arose for us. Our knowledge may be as slender as that of the thief on the cross (Luke 23:42); yet he had enough faith to be saved" (Anthony A. Hoekema, *Saved by Grace* [Grand Rapids, MI: Eerdmans Publishing Company, 1989], pp. 141-142).

14. Warren's remark in T*he Purpose-Driven Life* is virtually identical to what he said from the pulpit in his "What Time Is Christmas?" message: "You may be Catholic, you may be Jewish, you may be Presbyterian, or Buddhist, or Baptist, Lutheran....I don't care what your religious background is. God did not come to give you religion. He came to give you a relationship." (Similar statements commonly appear in Warren's sermons.)

15. A.W. Tozer, *The Pursuit of Man,* p. 60. Quoted in Marilynne E. Foster, *Tozer on the Holy Spirit: A 366-Day Devotional* (Camp Hill, PA: Christian Publications, 2000), under Jan. 2.

16. Tom Holladay and Kay Warren, "Why Doctrine Matters to Your Members," *MinistryToolBox,* June 30, 2004, issue #161, online at pastors.com.

17. Staff, "Biblical Doctrine Is Practical and Life-Changing," www.pastors.com/article.asp?ArtID=7006.

18. Larry Spargimino, *What You Need to Know About the Purpose-Driven Church* (Bethany, OK: Southwest Radio Bible Church, 2004), p. 4. Spargimino does not even cite Warren to prove his accusation, but instead, simply quotes another critic's opinion.

19. Rick Warren, *The Purpose-Driven Life*, p. 87.

20. Rick Warren, "How Jesus Replaced What Adam Erased," part 13, n.d.

21. Rick Warren, "Why Do I Do What I Don't Want to Do?" part 2, Nov. 1, 1998; "What We Believe: Who Is Man?" www.saddleback.com/flash/believe2.html; Rick Warren, "The Passion: The Rest of the Story," Easter 2004.

22. Rick Warren, *The Purpose-Driven Life*, pp. 86, 117.

23. "What We Believe: Who Is God?" www.saddleback.com/flash/believe2.html.

24. Tom Holladay and Kay Warren, *Foundations: 11 Core Truths to Build Your Life On* (Grand Rapids, MI: Zondervan, 2003), p. 101.

25. Casey Ryan, "A Review of *The Purpose-Driven Life*," www.aomin.org/PDL.html.

26. The "five points" of Calvinism are Total deprevity of man, Unconditional election, Limited atonement, Irrestible grace, and Perseverance of the saints (T.U.L.I.P.).

27. Tom Holladay, author's informal discussion, April 25, 2005.

28. "What We Believe: If I Accept Jesus Christ Is My Salvation Forever?" www.saddleback.com/flash/believe2.html.

29. Frances Swaggart, "The Cross of Christ: False Doctrine," *The Evangelist,* Mar. 2005, p. 32.

30. Rick Warren, "The Purpose of Preaching," part 2, Preaching Conference, n.d. He specifically mentions repentance in *The Purpose-Driven Life* on pages 105 and 182.

31. Rick Warren, "How to Communicate to Change Lives," part 1, session 3, 1997 (endnote also applicable to the quotes in the next paragraph of the main text).

32. Advertisement for *The Cross of Christ: False Doctrine* by Jimmy Swaggart, in *The Evangelist,* Mar. 2005, p. 12.

33. Rick Warren, *The Purpose-Driven Life*, pp. 58,78-79,112,162-163.

34. Francis Swaggart, "Tolerance at the Expense of Truth," *The Evangelist,* Mar. 2005, p. 14.

35. Rick Warren, "Maintaining Moral Purity," part 8, May 25, 1997.

36. Rick Warren, "Attracting a Crowd to Worship" (PDL Conference).

37. John MacArthur, interview, "The Purpose-Driven Life," *Newsnight* (CNN), Mar. 16, 2005.

38. Rick Warren, "Building on My Strengths: The Purpose-Driven Life," part 3, May 9, 1993.

## Chapter 5: A New Spirituality?

1. Rick Warren, "Developing Trust," part 3, Apr. 20, 1997.

2. This accusation has appeared in many forms and in countless places.

3. James Sundquist, *Who's Driving the Purpose-Driven Church?* (Bethany, OK: Rock Salt Publishing, 2004), p. 87.

4. Larry Spargimino, *What You Need to Know About the Purpose-Driven Church* (Bethany, OK: Southwest Radio Bible Church, 2004), pp. 15-16.

5. Tim Challies, "Rick Warren," Nov. 3, 2004, online at www.challies.com.

6. This accusation has appeared in many forms and in countless places.

7. Rick Warren, "The Good News Is for Everybody!," part 26, n.d.; Rick Warren, "Discovering Life Mission," C.L.A.S.S. 401.

8. Richard Abanes, "Cults & Students: Ten Cults Seeking Converts" and "Cults & Your Family: A Clear and Present Danger," Purpose-Driven Youth Conference.

9. Matt Costella, "An Analysis of Rick Warren's The Purpose-Driven Life," online at www.fundamentalbiblechurch.org.

10. Rick Warren, "Developing Trust," part 3, Apr. 20, 1997.

11. Elliot Miller, *A Crash Course on the New Age Movement* (Grand Rapids, MI: Zondervan, 1991; 1992 edition), p. 17.

12. Warren Smith, *Deceived on Purpose* (Magalia, CA: Mountain Stream Press, 2004), pp. 17, 62, 137; Frances Swaggart, "Testing the Spirits," *The Evangelist,* Feb. 2005, p. 32.

13. Rick Warren, "Discovering Church Membership," C.L.A.S.S. 101.

14. Rick Warren, "The Task Before Us Is Enormous, but God Is Equipping Us," Mar. 30, 2005, *MinistryToolBox,* issue #200, online at www.pastors.com

15. Spargimino, pp. 29-30.

16. Swaggart, p. 13.

17. Rick Warren, "Where Is God When You Need Him?" part 2, Feb. 14, 1988.

18. Rick Warren, "Developing Trust," part 3, Apr. 20, 1997.

19. Rick Warren, *The Purpose-Driven Life* (Grand Rapids, MI: Zondervan, 2002), p. 172.

20. Despite Saddleback's rejection of pantheism, some critics have even sought to prove the church's pantheistic and New Age leanings by drawing attention to the Foundations classes by Kay Warren and Tom Holladay (see p. 78). Their course mentions that God is "immanent," adding that God is "within and throughout his creation" (Tom Holladay and Kay Warren, *Foundations: 11 Core Truths to Build Your Life On,* participant's guide [Grand Rapids, MI: Zondervan, 2003], p. 46.) Although such language reflects a perfectly orthodox way of referring to God's attribute of immanence, Kay and Tom unfortunately listed their section under the innocuous heading "A Fresh Word." Why unfortunately?

Because the word "fresh" just happens to also appear in the 1948 New Age book *The Reappearance of the Christ* (republished in 2002) by occult Theosophist Alice Bailey (1880–1949). Bailey talked about "a fresh orientation to divinity." The critic reasoned that since Bailey used "fresh" and Kay Warren and Tom Holladay used "fresh"—and Bailey was a pantheist—then Warren and Holladay must be pantheists, too, as is Rick Warren, who has already proven as much since he said God is "in" everything (see Smith, pp. 156-157).

But the Warrens (and Holladay) are only saying that since God is omnipresent we always have access to Him. As Rick Warren says, "Because God is with you all the time, no place is any closer to God than the place where you are right now (Rick Warren, *The Purpose-Driven Life,* p. 88). (Interestingly, before their "fresh" comment in the "Participant's Guide," Holladay and Kay Warren spent five pages explaining the historic, orthodox view of the Trinity. The "Teacher's Guide" contains ten full pages of discussion points to teach regarding classic Trinitarian theology. All of these pages, however, were ignored by the critic.)

21. This was the assessment made by Jon Walker, vice-president of Purpose-Driven Ministries, who in an April 12, 2005, letter referred to Warren Smith as follows: "[Ex-cultists] are naturally sensitive to the danger of deception and sometimes begin to see evidence of cult belief in places where it simply does not exist. They read their own experiences into other people's lives and attribute cult meanings to words and phrases when the authors in fact are using them in the ordinary ways used by people who have no cult connection....When Mr. Smith finds 'evidence' of New Age beliefs in *The Purpose-Driven Life,* he is reading his own past cult beliefs into it—without regard for what Pastor Rick actually is saying."

22. T.A. McMahon, "The Purpose-Driven Life: A Critique," pp. 6-7.

23. Contemplative prayer (also known as "centering prayer") is controversial but does not *necessarily* border on occultism and Eastern meditation (though some of its proponents have drawn from non-Christian forms of meditation). It is supposed to be Trinitarian and Christ-centered; it is meant to help people slow down from the daily rat race and be still and quiet before God with the earnest expectation of hearing Him speak to their soul.

This is accomplished by removing distraction from the mind and centering one's thoughts on God. It is a prayer of silence whereby a Christian experiences the infinite majesty and wonder of the Lord while simultaneously realizing how close He is to each of us as the very source of all we are and all we can be.

Acceptable forms of this prayer method should *not* conform to New Age meditation practices, which are meant to bring about an altered state of consciousness whereby one is "enlightened" to the so-called truths of self-divinity and the oneness of all that is (pantheism).

Any Christian who has ever gazed silently at a mountain range or stared quietly at the ocean in awe of God, desiring that He would speak to them in the stillness, has come very close to practicing contemplative prayer (see Mike

Perschon, "Desert Youth Worker: Disciplines, Mystics, and the Contemplative Life," *Youth Worker*, Nov./Dec. 2004, online at www.youthspecialties.com).

24. A.W. Tozer, *The Warfare of the Spirit*, pp. 95-96. Quoted in Marilynne E. Foster, *Tozer on the Holy Spirit: A 366-Day Devotional* (Camp Hill, PA: Christian Publications, 2000), under Jan. 1.

25. Consider these quotes: "Not to advance in the spiritual life is to go back"; "There is not in the world a kind of life more sweet and delightful, than that of a continual conversation with God"; "We cannot escape the dangers which abound in life, without the actual and continual help of God; let us then pray to Him for it continually" (Brother Lawrence, *Practicing the Presence of God*, online at http://prayerfoundation.org).

26. C. Peter Williams, "Brother Lawrence," in J.D. Douglas, gen. ed., *The New International Dictionary of the Christian Church* (Grand Rapids, MI: Zondervan, 1974; 1978 ed.), p. 158.

27. Rick Warren, *The Purpose-Driven Life*, pp. 87-88.

28. Rick Warren, *The Purpose-Driven Life*, p. 89.

29. "Breviary," in Samuel MaCauley Jackson, editor-in-chief, *The New Schaff-Herzog Encyclopedia of Religious Knowledge* (Grand Rapids, MI: Baker Book House), p. 263.

30. Spargimino, pp. 18-19; Sundquist, p. 35; Albert James Dager, review of *Deceived on Purpose*, in *Media Spotlight*, vol. 27, no. 3, online at www.erwm.com; "Has Your Church Adopted the Purpose-Driven Life Agenda?" www.scionofzion.com/toc.htm. Further false comments that have been made in this vein include the following: "[L]et us consider Schuller's followers like Bill Hybels and Rick Warren" (Bob DeWaay, "Redefining the Church," *Critical Issues Commentary*, Nov./Dec. 2004, issue 85, online at www.twincityfellowship.com); "Warren, who went to (guess where) The Robert Schuller Bible College" ("Billy Graham," online at www.apostasyrevealed.com); "[Warren] has surrounded himself with such questionable folk and questionable counsel as Peter Drucker (a known New Ager), Robert Schuller (a Known New Ager)" ("A Letter to a Houston Area Church that Is in the Process of Changing from a Conventional Baptist Church to a 'Purpose-Driven Church,'" online at www.cephas-library.com); "[Warren] has been heavily influenced by Positive Thinking guru Robert Schuller" (Albert James Dager, review of *Deceived on Purpose*, in *Media Spotlight*, vol. 27, no. 3, online at www.erwm.com); "[I cannot] understand why any Bible believer could follow men such as Bill Hybels, John Maxwell and Rick Warren, when they are speaking for a man like Schuller" (E.L. Bynum, "Hybels and Schuller Back Together Again," http://bz.llano.net/baptist/pbc007.htm).

31. Tim Stafford, "A Regular Purpose-Driven Guy," *Christianity Today*, Nov. 18, 2002, online at www.ctlibrary.com.

32. Rick Warren, "Handling a Failure in Your Ministry" (Leadership Lifter), n.d.; Rick Warren, "How to Communicate Your Vision" (Leadership Lifter), n.d.

33. Rick Warren, "Targeting Your Community: Understanding Who You Are Trying to Reach," c. 1997. Other extremely rare references to Schuller by Warren have been 1) a 1985 sermon in which he cites Schuller's harmless opinion that people should "make the best of a bad situation"; 2) a 1987 sermon wherein he refers to the oft-repeated Schullerism "Tough times never last; tough people do"; 3) a 1989 sermon in which he borrows Schuller's line "God wants to turn your scars into stars," which he used to illustrate the biblical truth that God can and does heal our emotional wounds when we come to Him—no matter how deeply we have been scarred by the world and sin (see Rick Warren, "Letting Go of Loneliness," part 5, Dec. 8, 1985; "How To Develop Staying Power," part 7, June 7, 1987; "Healing Scars of Shattered Confidence," part 3, Apr. 9, 1989).

34. Robert Schuller, "What Will Be the Future of This Ministry?" message delivered by Schuller from the pulpit of the Crystal Cathedral, *Hour of Power*, April 4, 2004.

35. See "Rick Warren" and "Robert Schuller," online at www.myfortress.org

## Chapter 6: Exaltation of Self?

1. Respectively: Mac Dominick, *Rebuilding the Tower of Babel* (Lexington, SC: Cutting Edge Ministries, 2005), available for purchase at www.cuttingedge.org; Standing in the Gap Ministries, "Here Are Some Observations," www.antiosas .org/Warren1.htm; steenkeenbadges, Internet message board post, Mar. 24, 2005, online at www.freerepublic.com; Robert Jenkins, "Rick Warren and Bill Hybels: Men of God or Dangerous Hucksters?" online at www.observations.net; Richard Bennett, "The Adulation of Man in The Purpose-Driven Life," online at www.monergism.com.

2. Larry Spargimino, *What You Need to Know About The Purpose-Driven Church* (Bethany, OK: Southwest Radio Church Ministries, 2004), p. 3.

3. Rick Warren, *The Purpose-Driven Life* (Grand Rapids, MI: Zondervan, 2002), p. 231.

4. Phil Callaway "Interview with Rick Warren," *Servant*, Fall 2002, www.christian ity.ca/faith/christian-living/2004/03.000.html.

5. Warren, *The Purpose-Driven Life*, p. 306.

6. A.W. Tozer, *The Pursuit of Man*, p. 164. Quoted in Marilynne E. Foster, *Tozer on the Holy Spirit: A 366-Day Devotional* (Camp Hill, PA: Christian Publications, 2000), under Jan. 2.

7. A.W. Tozer, *That Incredible Christian*. Quoted in Edythe Draper, comp., *The Pursuit of God and The Pursuit of Man: Devotional Readings* (Camp Hill, PA: Christian Publications, 2002), p. 2 of *The Pursuit of Man* section.

8. T.A. McMahon, "The Purpose-Driven Life: A Critique," p. 7.

9. Warren, *The Purpose-Driven Life*, pp. 89, 103.

10. Charles F. Pfeiffer and Everett F. Harrison, eds., *The Wycliffe Bible Commentary* (Chicago: Moody Press, 1962; 1985 ed.), p. 939.

11. Spargimino, p. 31.

12. Warren, *The Purpose-Driven Life,* p. 41.

13. Rick Warren, "Developing Trust." Warren also has said, "When war happens, there are casualties. So we're to pray and trust God, realizing that *God is in control*" (Rick Warren, "What Does the Bible Say About War?" *MinistryToolBox,* Aug. 28, 2002, issue #65, online at www.pastors.com).

14. Rick Warren, "It All Starts with God," Dec. 25, 2002, *MinistryToolBox,* issue #82, online at www.pastors.com.

15. Spargimino, p. 10.

16. Rick Warren, *The Purpose-Driven Church* (Grand Rapids, MI: Zondervan, 1995), pp. 397, 83.

17. Warren, *The Purpose-Driven Church,* pp. 255-256.

18. See Gordon Miller, "The Church Service Question," *Leadership Letter,* July/Aug. 2003, p. 3, www.carey.ac.nz/leadership/pdf/177.pdf.

19. See S. Klein, "Drucker as Business Moralist," *Journal of Business Ethics,* #28, p. 121; "Peter Drucker's Search for Community," *Business Week Online,* Dec. 24, 2002; cf. "Ken Witty on Creating a Documentary on Management Expert Peter Drucker"; "Reason for Creating a Documentary on Drucker"; "Lessons Learned from Drucker"; and "Views by Drucker on Workers" (available from Orange County Public Library "Business Source Premier" database); Jacques Maritain, *Reflections of America* (New York: Charles Scribner's Sons, 1958, online ed.), endnote 65 in "Reflections in America III," www.nd.edu/ Departments/Maritain/ etext/reflect3.html; Peter Drucker, *The End of Economic Man* (London: Transaction Publishers, 1995 rep.), pp. 87-103;

20. Tim Stafford, "Business of the Kingdom," *Christianity Today,* online at www.ct library.com.

21. Rich Karlgaard, "Real-World Advice for the Young," Apr. 11, 2005, *Forbes,* vol. 175, Issue 7, Orange County Public Library "Business Source Premier" database; Patricial B. Dailey, "CEO Style," *Restaurants & Institutions,* July 1, 2004, vol. 114, issue 15, p. 10, Orange County Public Library "Business Source Premier" database; Dick Gorelick, "An Explanation of My Business Philosophy," *American Printer,* Apr. 2003, vol. 231, issue 1, p. 58, Orange County Public Library "Business Source Premier" database (this quote is Gorelick's paraphrase of Drucker's general philosophy of business).

22. A. Shaker Zahra, "An Interview with Peter Drucker," *Academy of Management Executive,* Aug. 2003, vol. 17, issue 3, p. 9 (Orange County Public Library "Business Source Premier" database); and, as quoted in Stafford.

23. Peter Drucker, *Landmarks of Tomorrow*. Quoted in Jack Beatty, *The World According to Peter Drucker* (New York: Broadway Books, 1998), p. 98.

24. Spargimino, pp. 5-6.

25. Rich Karlgaard, "Peter Drucker on Leadership," Nov. 19, 2004, online at www.for bes.com.

26. See Peter Drucker, "The Unfashionable Kierkegaard," *Sewanee Review*, Oct./Dec. 1949, pp. 587-602.

27. Peter Drucker, *Post-Capitalist Society* (New York: HarperCollins, 1993), p. 13.

28. Warren, *The Purpose-Driven Life*, pp. 72, 78, 118; "What We Believe," www.pastors .com/pcom/subscriptions/whatwebelieve.asp.

29. Rick Warren, untitled sermon, Laguna Hills High School, May 20, 1984, reprinted in *25-Day Family Devotional* (Lake Forest, CA: Saddleback Church, 2005), under Apr. 5.

30. "Purpose-Driven Communities," www.purposedriven.com/en-US/Communities/ Community_Home.htm.

31. Casey Ryan, "A Review of *The Purpose-Driven Life,*" www.aomin.org/PDL.html.

32. Rick Warren, *The Purpose-Driven Life*, p. 24.

33. Millard J. Erickson, *God in Three Persons: A Contemporary Interpretation of the Trinity* (Grand Rapids, MI: Baker Books, 1995), pp. 221-222; Rick Warren, *The Purpose-Driven Life*, p. 24.

34. Warren, *The Purpose-Driven Life*, p. 232.

35. Todd Wilken, "Purpose-Driven or Forgiveness-Driven?" online at www.issuesetc .org. Wilken is host of the radio talk show *Issues, Etc.* (Lutheran Church, Missouri Synod).

36. Warren, *The Purpose-Driven Life*, pp. 72, 76.

37. James Sundquist, *Who's Driving the Purpose-Driven Church?* (Bethany, OK: Rock Salt Publishing, 2004), p. 46.

38. Warren, *The Purpose-Driven Life*, p. 314.

39. An overemphasis on word similarities is a very dubious type of argumentation. One of Warren's critics, for instance, condemns his use of *The Message* paraphrase of the Bible, saying, "[It] changes the word 'Lord,' when used in reference to Jesus Christ, to 'Master,' a common New Age designation" (Spargimino, p. 11).

But such scrutiny also can be turned against the classic King James Version of the Bible (KJV), which also translates the Greek word *kurios* (normally rendered *Lord*) as *Master* in reference to Jesus (see Ephesians 6:9 and Colossians 4:1). Is the KJV now New Age?

Consider, too, the KJV's use of *unicorn* in Deuteronomy 33:17, Job 39:9, Psalm 92:10, Isaiah 34:7, and Numbers 23:22. This word is not in the Hebrew text, which reads *re'em* (or "wild ox"). So, should we assume that the true Hebrew word was ignored by corrupt KJV translators—pagans who chose to follow the Greek Septuagint's use of the word *monokeros* ("one-horn") and deceptively substituted that word for *re'em*, which resulted in the the translation *unicorn?* If so, this would mean that the KJV is *really* a New Age Bible version—and that anyone who uses it is a New Ager. Unicorns, after all, are not even real. They are mystical creatures that must be conjured up in the imagination through New Age visualization...just like a demon is conjured up through a spell. And unicorns are often found as New Age decorations and used as symbols for New Age groups. Clearly, taking word similarities to an extreme as a method of critical analysis is without any merit.

40. Nathan Busenitz, "A Sense of Purpose: Evaluating the Claims of the Purpose-Driven Life," online at www.gty.org.

41. Brandon, "What Is Church Anyway?" Internet message board post, Dec. 17, 2004, http://blog.badchristian.com/blogs/index.php/2004/12/.

42. Rick Warren, *The Purpose-Driven Life,* pp. 29, 50, 178, 267.

43. Dan Norcini, "Critique of the 'Seeker-Sensitive, Purpose Driven' Church Method," Sovereign Grace Bible Church, www.agetwoage.org/PDC.htm.

44. Rick Warren, *The Purpose-Driven Life,* pp. 58, 79, 86, 105, 112, 132, 198, 288, 294.

45. Greg Koukl, "What's Wrong with Being Seeker-Centered?" *Stand to Reason* commentary, online at www.str.org.

46. Rick Warren, "The Foundation for Happiness: Exploding The Myths That Make Us Miserable," Aug. 21, 1994.

47. Tom Holladay, "What Happens After I Die?" part 5, May 24, 1992.

48. Rick Warren, "The Passion: The Rest of the Story," Easter sermon, 2004.

"An insightful, helpful, and tactful presentation of Mormonism."
DR. NORMAN GEISLER

A Closer Look at
21st-Century Mormonism

Becoming
Gods

Richard
Abanes

# Becoming Gods

*A Closer Look at 21st-Century Mormonism*
Richard Abanes

Did you know Mormons hope to eventually become gods?

This and other Latter-day Saint doctrines can lead to misunderstanding and conflict when you interact with Mormon friends, neighbors, and co-workers. If you find yourself confused by their religion—a religion that has increasingly come to resemble mainstream Christianity—you're not alone.

Richard Abanes' thorough yet accessible approach helps you understand not only what today's Mormons believe, but also how they think about and defend their faith. The award-winning journalist offers the results of his research into many key teachings and beliefs, such as—

- who God is, who Jesus is, and what it means for us to participate in their divine nature

- why Joseph Smith and his visions have such a central place in the hearts of Mormons

- what role the Book of Mormon and other authoritative writings play in LDS beliefs

- how Mormons are now dealing with evangelicals' criticisms of their faith

- how you can effectively talk to 21st-century Mormons about their religion

*Becoming Gods* shows you how to weigh Mormonism's ever-changing claims...as well as how you can graciously live out God's love in your interactions with members of The Church of Jesus Christ of Latter-day Saints.

*"An insightful, helpful, and tactful presentation of Mormonism."*
—Dr. Norman Geisler

## Harry Potter, Narnia, and The Lord of the Rings

*What You Need to Know*
*About Fantasy Books and Movies*
Richard Abanes

Fantasy can help children see with spiritual eyes, says Richard Abanes, bestselling author of *Harry Potter and the Bible*. It confirms the reality of good and evil. But is every fantasy story appropriate for everyone?

In this evenhanded exploration of the books of J.K. Rowling, C.S. Lewis, and J.R.R. Tolkien, as well as the films based on their writings, Abanes—a fantasy fan himself—answers key questions:

- What is inspiring and healthy in these works? What is misleading and harmful?
- Do I need to be concerned about occult influence from fantasy?
- How do movies and merchandising impact kids' minds?

Pro-literature and pro-fun, *Harry Potter, Narnia, and The Lord of the Rings* helps you evaluate fantasy's strengths and dangers from a balanced Christian perspective.

*"Informative...a great resource for parents!"*
—Bill Myers, bestselling youth and children's fiction author